Vol. LVI No. 2, Magazine No. 221

Appalachia

▲ Est. 1876   America's Longest-Running Journal of Mountaineering & Conservation

Appalachian Mountain Club
Boston, Massachusetts

AMC MISSION

Founded in 1876, the Appalachian Mountain Club, a nonprofit organization with more than 90,000 members, promotes the protection, enjoyment, and wise use of the mountains, rivers, and trails of the Appalachian region. We believe that the mountains and rivers have an intrinsic worth and also provide recreational opportunity, spiritual renewal, and ecological and economic health for the region. We encourage people to enjoy and appreciate the natural world because we believe that successful conservation depends on this experience.

Appalachia is published by the AMC from its publications office at 5 Joy Street, Boston, Massachusetts, 02108. ISSN 0003-6587 ISBN 1-929173-99-7 Third-class postage paid at Boston, Massachusetts, and other mailing offices. The Journal is issued 2 times a year: Summer/Fall issue (June 15) and Winter/Spring issue (December 15). A subscription (both issues) is $15 for one year, $26 for two years, $33 for three years.

 Printed on recycled paper with soy-content ink.

These boots are made for White Mountain walking. See the story of the legendary Limmer boot in this issue's Mountain Voices, page 86.

Appalachia

▲ Est. 1876 America's Longest-Running Journal of Mountaineering & Conservation

Editor's Note: There was an error on page 12 of the Summer/Fall 2005 issue of *Appalachia*. In the "AMC's Maine Woods Initiative" article, Governor John Baldacci is referred to as James Baldacci. We apologize for the error.

Title page photo: *A view of Webster Cliffs from Mt. Willey.* PHOTO BY KEVIN ROONEY

Front cover photo: *A summit fox enjoys a quiet February day on the Rockpile.*
PHOTO BY JIM SALGE, MT. WASHINGTON OBSERVATORY

Back cover photo: *A rack of Limmer boots.*
PHOTO BY NED THERRIEN, NORTH STAR PHOTOGRAPHY

In This Issue

page 48

page 54

page 86

Leaving the Journal But Not the Pack

L AST SUMMER, THE MOUNTAINEERS BOOKS SENT ME A REMARKABLE book, *Living with Wolves*, by filmmakers Jim and Jamie Dutcher. Reading about the Dutchers' six-year experience observing the behavior of North American gray wolves, I was drawn to the way the couple had approached these animals—with intelligence, care, and respect, but without misguided reverence. They created a huge wilderness enclosure in Idaho's Sawtooth Mountains and, through trial and error, succeeded in forming a cohesive pack to live there. What began as a two-year film project expanded to six. Two award-winning films grew out of this experiment, and in the end, the animals—who had grown too used to humans to survive in the wild—were moved to protected areas.

From their years of living with one pack of wolves, the Dutchers shape wise observations about the leaderly qualities of the alphas, the supportive role of the betas, and the resourcefulness of my own favorites, the beleaguered omegas, least in stature but certainly not in impact. Though the Dutchers develop a deep affection for the members of the Sawtooth Pack, they do not romanticize the wolves into "spirit animals," and warn against treating these fierce canines like man's best friend. This measured approach allows the wolves to emerge, simply, as who they are. "This is the wolf that we want to share," they write, "a wolf that is neither demon nor deity nor biological robot. It is an animal that desperately needs to be part of something bigger than itself—the pack."

While I was reading *Living with Wolves*, I was also preparing my last *Appalachia* manuscript and inevitably thinking back on what has been an enjoyable and meaningful six-year tenure as this journal's editor. I was puzzled at first by the strong response I was having to the book, and then I came upon the photograph that appears (through the generosity of the authors) on the opposite page. Paw in hand, hand in paw, it is a portrait of connection. If I had to pick one gift that this journal has given me during the past six years, it is a heightened awareness of all that connects me to something bigger than myself, all that expands my pack to include others—both human and non-, and the landscape itself.

PHOTO BY JIM DUTCHER, COURTESY OF THE MOUNTAINEERS BOOKS

Some of this heightened awareness has come from my contact with outdoor lovers around the world, who have shared their own connections to the land with me and in these pages. Some of it has come from the collaborations I have enjoyed with the great people who worked with me on *Appalachia*, especially the knowledgeable, dedicated section editors who widen the journal's reach through Alpina, Accidents, News and Notes, Books of Note, and Poetry.

And some of my enhanced sense of connection has come from the work of shaping the stories themselves. I brought to the journal a love of the outdoors and a commitment to preserving wilderness. Then, when *Appalachia* became a part of my life, I found myself becoming more mindful during my outdoor wanderings, more responsive to the impossible delicacy of trillium along rugged trails, to the many colors I can find in a gray rock, to the enviably long eyelashes of the seal flirting with my kayak, to the sun-warmed skin of a plump blueberry, to the transparent beech leaf hanging tenaciously to an ice-coated branch, to the bear and moose and coyote and fox whose pawprints dart across my own in the New Hampshire hills.

Throughout its long history of celebrating both recreation and conservation, this journal has sought to portray the natural world as "neither demon nor deity nor biological robot" but rather as a place of enjoyment and responsibility, a place of essential links and critical interdependence. As the Dutchers so artfully point out, there is no such thing as a lone wolf. *Appalachia* has helped me understand that—whether alpha, beta, or omega—we all have a vital role to play in "the family of things."*

—*Lucille Stott*
Editor-in-Chief

*The phrase ends Mary Oliver's poem "Wild Geese."

In Grizzly Country

The Wonders and Hazards of Hiking Alaska's Brooks Range

By Mark Goodreau

O N MY FIRST TRIP TO BETTLES, A JUMPING-OFF POINT FOR HIKES into the Gates of the Arctic National Park in the central Brooks Range, I waited four gloomy days for the skies to clear before abandoning my plans to hike. Weather is fickle in the Arctic. Some August days are warm and sunny; more often it rains, with low clouds shrouding the mountaintops, making flights into and out of the Brooks Range treacherous. Occasionally, there is even snow. Running out of time, I traveled south and saw Denali and the Alaska Range instead, a wonderful consolation, but not the place I wanted most to explore. So, I was understandably anxious to board the floatplane in Bettles on my next visit, before being grounded by a different kind of flight hazard.

Alaska's boreal forest was on fire in the summer of 2004, and thick smoke drifted north across the Arctic Circle. On the flight up from Fairbanks, we saw great columns of smoke in every direction, rising from the charred remains of spruce trees. Fairbanks, itself, was engulfed in it, suffocating and claustrophobic. Thankfully, the smoke thinned out by the time we reached Bettles Airfield late in the morning. Still, we waited two hours for conditions to improve before receiving the tentative go-ahead from Brooks Range Aviation.

While the four of us prepared to board a Beaver floatplane, Bill, our pilot, checked his radio for last-minute reports from others already in the air. The news was disheartening: persistent haze in the valleys west and north was hampering visibility. "Maybe we should wait," said Bill, as if testing the idea with the group. I fought back nightmare visions of spending another four days stuck in the hangar at the Bettles field, praying for blue skies. After a few tense minutes of talking and weighing risks, it was finally time to go.

Our guide, David van den Berg, packed his two huskies in back of the Beaver with the remainder of our gear. The dogs, Lucky and Tussock, were coming along to help carry our food. David had traveled to Alaska from Florida after college to help clean up the Exxon *Valdez* mess and fell in love

Guide David van den Berg with his dog, Lucky, in the central Brooks Range.

with the wilderness. He'd been guiding trips into the far north ever since, first as a hired hand, and then as the owner of Arctic Wild, Inc. Joining us on this trip were two other clients: Jesse May, a pharmaceutical researcher from Fort Worth, Texas; and Claudia Klingbeil, a young Swiss woman, who was working for an adventure travel outfitter in Bettles for the summer. We were all excited to be on our way, except for four-year-old brothers Tussock and Lucky, who were terrified of planes.

We flew slowly away from Bettles, crossing the Alatna foothills to the west, and then angled northwest through the Alatna River valley. Sitting next to Bill in the cramped cockpit, I watched the Brooks Range rise up and surround us, mountains as far as we could see and beyond. Rolling hills gave way to rocky peaks, with the highest summits on the distant horizon capped in snow and ice. The lower summits and mountainsides were covered with a thin mantle of vegetation, mostly in shades of green and beige, with patches of yellow in the valleys. Autumn, which usually begins in late August in this part of the Arctic, was arriving late this year after the hot summer, and only the river willows had changed color. Passing north of the invisible tree line, above the open tundra, Bill pointed to sporadic movement below: Dall's sheep, white as cotton, clumped together on a mountain ridge; a moose cow and calf splashing across a stream; caribou trickling south. Soon we'd be walking among them.

Gates of the Arctic National Park is the most remote and least visited national park in America, with only 5,000 visitors a year in an area the size of Massachusetts and Connecticut combined. Gates of the Arctic is also the central component of a 40-million-acre reserve, the largest protected wilderness on the planet. Development has been encroaching on this landscape, and pressure for further development is increasing with the Trans-Alaska oil pipeline to the east, Prudhoe Bay and the petroleum reserves north, coal and other mining concessions north and south. For now, it remains mostly pristine.

The Brooks Range, the northernmost major mountain system in the world, runs through the park and past its borders, west to the Chukchi Sea and east to Canada's Yukon. The park is also source of six of the country's Wild and Scenic Rivers, including the Noatak, longest and wildest of them all. And the entire ecosystem provides habitat for the Western Arctic caribou herd, the largest in Alaska. It is a superlative landscape.

John Kauffman of the National Park Service, chief planner for Gates of the Arctic NP, envisioned this place as the ultimate destination for wilderness seekers. A "black-belt park," he called it, with "no roads, no trails, no bridges, no campgrounds, no interpretive signs, none of the woodsy aids and conveniences with which most parks are equipped." For practical reasons, most visitors use the air taxi service in Bettles to get in and out of the immense park. Once inside, though, you're on your own.

We camped the first day near our drop-off point at Lake Matcharak on the Noatak River, placing five tents strategically on dry islands in the soppy tundra, one a mess tent for eating and storing food safely away from our beds. Our plan was to walk cross-country fifty miles in twelve days back to the Alatna River, on a northeast course roughly perpendicular to the fall migration route of the caribou. We carried everything on our backs: sixty-five pounds each of food, cookware, fuel, tents, clothing, and other personal gear. David also carried a satellite phone for emergencies and a short-range radio to communicate with the bush pilots on pick-up. The dogs, Lucky and Tussock, carried twenty pounds each. The idea was to transfer some of our weight to the dogs as they ate down their own food supply so that they would maintain a constant twenty pounds each for the entire journey. They would help us lighten our packs more quickly.

By late afternoon the first caribou appeared, in small bands of ten to twenty animals. A mixture of bulls, cows, and calves spilled periodically across the northern hills into the broad Noatak Valley. The prominent bulls pranced across the tundra, noses pointed up in the air, balancing their impressive antlers on thick muscular necks. Stopping only briefly to graze, they moved restlessly southwards. The Western Arctic herd, half a million strong, makes up ten percent of the world caribou population. In autumn, they migrate from the uplands north of the Brooks Range to their wintering grounds in the sparsely-treed tundra south of the Brooks, where their winter food is the tundra lichens. Fattened from summer's bounty, with full antlers and shiny new coats—tan with white chests and hindquarters—the bull caribou are in their prime. For the native Alaskans, the Inupiat and Athapascans, and the visiting sport hunters seeking trophies, this is also prime hunting season.

Hiking Among Grizzlies

In the early evening, a bear showed up on the hill behind camp. David spotted him first with binoculars, a half-mile distant, grazing on roots and berries, digging for small rodents. *Ursus arctos*, the grizzly bear, is also called the brown bear, but in reality the grizzly can be many shades of color, from blond to black. Smaller than the coastal bears of southern Alaska, which can attain 1,300 pounds on richer diets, the barren-ground grizzly of the Arctic tops out at 600 pounds. It takes a hundred square miles to support a grizzly on this land, which is fallow nine months of the year. I felt a mixture of fear and awe seeing this creature, and was glad to view him from a distance.

In his book *Coming into the Country*, John McPhee describes his exhilarating first encounter with the barren-ground grizzly:

> The sight of the bear stirred me like nothing else the country could contain. What mattered was not so much the bear himself as what the bear implied. He was the predominant thing in that country, and for him to be in it at all meant that there had to be more country like it in every direction and more of the same kind of country all around that. He implied a world.

Claudia, Jesse, and David at camp near Mount Papik. PHOTO BY MARK GOODREAU

Our first bear disappeared as night fell, but none of us saw him leave. In the arctic twilight, I slept lightly and listened apprehensively for the foraging grizzly, or the snorts and grunts of passing caribou. I heard only the haunting cry of a loon.

A cold front passed through the next day, bringing clouds and wind, then crystal skies. We walked nine tortuous miles shouldering heavy packs. Though the tundra is open and appears to be a groomed surface from a distance, the terrain is rough and difficult to cross in many places. Dense brush borders waterways and the lower hillsides, thick with willows, alders, and other dwarf trees. Tussock tundra, formed of cottongrass and other sedges, spoils much of the flatland for casual walking. These basketball-sized hummocks are covered in slick grass and surrounded by a spongy bog. When walking through tussock tundra, it is hard to maintain a rhythm, to keep balanced. We slipped and struggled and eventually reached a dry area near a small creek and made camp under Mount Papik, one of the few named peaks on the map.

On a layover day, blessed with clear skies and cool conditions, our four-some scaled Mount Papik for the 360-degree panorama. At 4,890 feet, neither high nor steep, the summit was nevertheless challenging to reach. With the top third of the mountain covered in crumbled shale, climbing Papik felt like scrambling up a pile of broken dinner plates. Our efforts were rewarded, though, with the kind of outlook that was once commonplace and that now few will ever see: miles of wilderness in every direction.

Bob Marshall exulted in these wild overlooks. A staff member of the U.S. Forest Service, Marshall spent a total of 210 days exploring the Brooks Range on four trips from 1929 to 1939, and was an early champion of conservation in the region. He coined the name Gates of the Arctic after two distinct mountains to the east, Boreal Mountain and Frigid Crags. Marshall thought he had discovered the high point of the Brooks Range as well, but that turned out to be farther north, Mount Isto at 9,060 feet. Most peaks are in the 5,000–7,000 foot range.

Though modest in elevation, the mountains are notable for their extraordinary and complex make-up. Metamorphic rocks form the highest summits, mixed in with bare granite and limestone peaks, all sculpted over eons by plate tectonics and a series of ice ages. Now the ice is gone, except for a few relict glaciers. But the handiwork is plainly visible: arêtes, cirques, tarns, moraines, and classic U-shaped valleys. It is a naked landscape, a convoluted jumble, raw and savagely beautiful.

Close Encounter

"A bear is coming!" called Claudia, as she hurried back to the gravel bar where Jesse, David, and I waited. I watched, horrorstruck, as a 500-pound adult grizzly emerged from the brush, only 100 yards away, running and closing steadily on Claudia. It was our third day in the park, on the far side of Papik. We had been passing through a valley, resting near a creek after lunch, and Claudia had just walked into the willows for some privacy.

When the bear saw the rest of our group after Claudia rejoined us, he suddenly stopped and stood on his hind legs to get a better look at the situation. Then he decided to come closer. Approaching slowly, the bear stopped on the north bank of the shallow, braided stream where we stood. He was only 100 feet away now, directly across from us.

"Get a good look," said David. I wasn't sure if he was talking to the three of us or to the grizzly, who was staring intently at the group, sizing us up. Feeling a little sick in the stomach, I instinctively avoided the bear's gaze.

We were four puny humans, armed only with our wits and four canisters of Counter Assault Bear Deterrent, facing a grizzly bear that could chase down an adult caribou and kill it with a single bite to the neck. David had already warned us that the Arctic grizzlies seemed more predatory in the fall, on an urgent mission to pack on calories before the long arctic winter. He'd also reassured us that there was no record of any group of four people ever attacked by a grizzly bear. We were statistically safe, which brought me no comfort or courage at the time.

Standing closely in a group, with arms raised high above our heads to make us appear bigger, we spoke in grave voices: "Hey, bear; leave us alone; go away!" Still, the bear lingered and watched us in a way that felt menacing, though was perhaps only curious.

David, at one point, leashed Lucky and Tussock to his backpack on the gravel. He did not want the dogs to draw an attack.

After what seemed minutes and was probably only seconds, in the strange way that time expands in such a crisis, the bear continued upstream. Just as I began to relax, the bear spun around and came back at us from a different angle, seemingly more determined this time. I reflexively popped the safety cap off my bear spray and heard the hiss of aerosol.

Grizzly attacks against people are rare and almost always defensive in nature. Such attacks usually involve a sow with cubs or an adult protecting a food cache. Surprised by people moving too quietly or carelessly in their territory, the bears attack only to neutralize a perceived threat—and will stop once that is accomplished. The best defense in these situations is to play dead until the bear leaves. Climbing a tree is also an option, though not in the Arctic.

Predatory attacks are untypical and demand a different response. If an unprovoked bear approaches you, it's best to stand up to the threat. Let the bear know that you literally will not lie down.

As the emboldened grizzly crossed the first braid of river, David clapped his hands and yelled loudly, walking aggressively toward the animal. If the bear wanted a fight, he now had one willing opponent. I stood behind with Jesse and Claudia and hoped for the best.

The standoff ended as suddenly as it began. The bear simply turned away and walked slowly up the embankment, never looking back at us. Minutes later, he was grazing on berries. We gathered our packs, crossed to the other side of the valley, and continued upstream, keeping a wary eye on the bear.

In all recorded travel in arctic Alaska, there are few reports of violent meetings with bears, aside from those between bear and hunter. Only one visitor to Gates of the Arctic NP has been killed; that was in August 1996, on the Noatak River. Ernie Johnson, who traveled much in the Brooks Range in the early twentieth century with Bob Marshall and others, had this to say. "I've never yet seen a bear that did anything except run away from me."

Aftermath

For the remainder of our journey, we spoke little of our encounter with the grizzly bear, but it was often on my mind. I became more alert and aware of my surroundings, and saw the remarkable landscape through fresh eyes. Walking through valleys, past lakes and across streams that may not have been visited by another person in years, if ever, I had no choice but to be firmly in the present.

Navigating by map alone, we walked short distances between campsites, stopping for a day of rest and exploration when it suited us. I got to know each of my companions better. The intimacy of our shared bear experience brought us closer. We were already united by our love for the land, and I'm sure we all believed that the risks posed by such adventures — exposure to bad weather, dangerous wildlife, or accident — were essential parts of the experience. Each of us also sought time alone to enjoy the rare gift of solitude, but we never strayed too far from the group.

On our way northeast, the landscape slowly changed, and the mountains grew more rugged as we approached the Continental Divide. We stuck to the riverbeds when we could, or climbed high up the steep hillsides, where centuries-old caribou trails cleared our path forward. Every new valley we entered seemed more striking than the last. Near the midpoint of our journey, we camped behind a small lake in a hanging valley, where Claudia and David braved the chilly water for an evening bath. Beyond the far shore, framed by smaller mountains, layers of high peaks were mirrored in the still waters. I imagined we were the first to ever camp there.

One day, while eating a lunch of cheese and crackers from inside an open tent, protected from a chilly rain, Claudia noticed Tussock staring at the opposite hillside. Following his gaze, we saw an adult grizzly, almost black in color, grazing head down across the slope. We stepped outside the tent, to alert the bear to our presence. Hearing strange sounds or smelling foreign scents, the bear stood upright for a moment and looked at us from across the stream. He bolted away, and I laughed nervously, out of relief.

The following day at dinnertime, from the same vantage point, we saw a lone wolf. Light grayish white in color, mysterious and silent, he sat and watched us from a hillside for ten minutes before slipping away. How many times had a wolf or grizzly spied upon us unknowingly?

Most days were less eventful, though no less fulfilling. We discovered more hidden valleys and climbed unnamed peaks. We watched the ancient caribou migration unfold and gathered ripe cranberries and blueberries at our feet. We caught arctic grayling from a clear cold stream. We felt a glimmer of what it must have been like for our ancestors to explore an untamed landscape. As we fell into our own peaceful rhythm, the days blended together.

Near the end of our journey, this sense of timelessness was gradually dispelled. One night we heard jet engines overhead; the next day I spotted human footprints in the gravel. We saw a floatplane cruising the Alatna River valley to pick up other parties and met up with a solo backpacker who was hungry for company. Wildlife sightings became more sporadic. When we reached our take-out position near Gaedeke Lake, we decided to fly out a half-day early, rather than risk delay from bad weather, which would leave us stranded with dwindling food supplies. We also preferred not to camp in sight of the cabin perched incongruously on the lakeshore.

On the return flight, we saw a new fire spreading over the central Brooks Range. The valleys were ablaze in autumn color: bright reds and oranges from dwarf birch, purples of blueberry, and cream-colored lichen and moss carpeted the lower slopes; dark greens of spruce contrasted with the golden hues of willow and cottonwood along the river edges. Bob Marshall wrote, "I don't know any colors so varied and brilliant as those of arctic autumn." A New Hampshire native and witness of many beautiful autumns, I was astonished by the fiery display.

An hour in the air, still only halfway back to Bettles, we floated over an island of granite peaks named the Arrigetch by the native Inupiat, which means "fingers of the hand extended." Shimmering in the low angle light, the Arrigetch looked otherworldly, polished silver stone carved in knife-edges and steeple points.

We kept flying over mountains as far as we could see, over a wild country with valleys yet to be explored, mountain peaks to be climbed, where man and grizzly bear might still meet for the first time.

Sources

Douglas H. Chadwick, *Exploring America's Wild & Scenic Rivers*, Washington D.C.: National Geographic Society, 2001.

Stephen Herrero, *Bear Attacks: Their Causes and Avoidance*, Guilford, CT: The Lyons Press, 2002.

John M. Kauffmann, *Alaska's Brooks Range: The Ultimate Mountains*, Seattle, WA: The Mountaineers Books, 1997.

Robert Marshall, *Alaska Wilderness: Exploring the Central Brooks Range*, Los Angeles: University of California Press, 1970.

John McPhee, *Coming into the Country*, New York: The Noonday Press, 1998.

E.C. Pielou, *A Naturalist's Guide to the Arctic*, Chicago: The University of Chicago Press, 1994.

MARK GOODREAU lives in his hometown of Portsmouth, New Hampshire, and works as a consultant, freelance writer, and outdoor photographer. Mark often hikes in the mountains and forests of northern New England, where he keeps a respectful distance from ornery moose.

Mushing in New England

From Commerce to Competition to Cooperation

By Sarah Jane Shangraw

ACROSS THE ICY LAKE AND BEYOND A SCREEN OF BARREN TREES, I note slight movement. A shadow skirts the shore, rounding its way closer. The first team of sled dogs is on its way. We strain our ears to hear the yelping, but catch only the drone of a far-off snowmobile. I jam my boots farther into the snow bank and steady myself for a clear view of the bulky snow dogs whipping by in a frenzy of barking, powder, and harnesses.

I plan to savor my first glimpses of a sled dog team in action before it races by and reenters the woods on the other side of the clearing.

The folks around me lapse into small talk, and I realize I'm the only one teetering on anticipation's edge for a moment of sled dog mayhem. Then I see why. A team quietly emerges from the woods and draws closer. Moving steadily but slowly, the sled bumps through, rather than glides over, the snow. The team approaches at a jogger's easy pace. The dogs are small and scraggly — not thick-limbed, furry huskies. It takes them ages to get to the other end of the clearing, and as they pass, I have plenty of time to examine each one. They wear little green booties, their long tongues loll about, and they seem unable to catch their breath, much less yelp in the excited fury I've been expecting.

How can these scrappy dogs pull a sled in a 100-mile race through the Maine wilderness? Is this even humane?

It turns out I had mushing all wrong. Later, the mushers will tell me my misguided expectations are not that unusual. And, yes, it is humane.

THE NEW ENGLAND MUSHING COMMUNITY, SUPPORTED BY A HISTORY of Chinook and husky breeding, active sled dog clubs, and a tightly managed racing schedule, is vibrant and healthy. If one event can represent the genesis of this community, it is the return to Wonalancet, New Hampshire, of Arthur T. Walden, who had been away for some years in the early part of the 20th century, prospecting in the Klondike Gold Rush.

In Alaska and the Yukon, Walden had known a world that relied on working sled dogs for the transportation of food, mail, freight, and people to remote mines and camps, just as native arctic peoples had relied on sled dogs for thousands of years. In 1909, the All-Alaska Sweepstakes Race marked the birth of dog sledding as an organized sport. That same year, William Goosak,

Opposite: An excited dog sled team start their run in Sandwich, New Hampshire.
PHOTO BY JERRY AND MARCY MONKMAN

PHOTO COURTESY OF THE RPPC COLLECTION OF SUSAN E. MURRAY

The summer after the first Eastern International Race in Berlin, New Hampshire, Walden's Chinook Kennel was decimated by a distemper outbreak. His entire winning team, with the exception of old Chinook himself, died in the outbreak. Walden is thought to have taken a break during the 1923 and 1924 seasons to breed back a new competitive team. Featured in this photo are the yearlings with their sire, Chinook in the lead in 1924. This race may have been considered a training excercise for their 1925 comeback.

a Russian fur trader, introduced the Siberian husky to Alaska. Many deemed the race's one team of Siberians too small to compete with the long-legged Alaskan dogs—Malamutes, Samoyeds, and what would later be known as Alaskan huskies. But the Siberians' agility and speed proved more important than bulk in the 408-mile race, and they took third place.

Arthur Walden grew enamored of the sport and, upon his return to New Hampshire, threw himself into establishing a team of his own. In the early 1920s, the Brown Paper Company of Berlin, New Hampshire, held a sled dog race near the Canadian border. The event brought attention to the sport and, in particular, to Walden's lead dog "Chinook," from whom he would create the breed of the same name.

Around the same time, Walden founded the New England Sled Dog Club, and hosted a visit by the famous Norwegian prospector-cum-musher, Leonhard Seppala. Though Seppala's first forays into dog sledding were strictly business—he learned Eskimo ways and used his dog teams to deliver mail and freight—he and most other mushers transformed their business into a sport as airplanes and road development changed transportation methods.

Seppala had made quite a name for himself in Alaska after his working sled dog teams participated in the famed 1925 Serum Run, a relay rescue effort to bring antitoxins to the remote town of Nome, Alaska, which was beleaguered by a diphtheria epidemic. Planes could not reach the interior town due to an extreme cold snap, so the serum was taken as far as possible by train, and the dog teams ran a cumulative 676 miles to finish the journey, saving the town. It is said that the Iditarod was established in honor of this run, though officially it is meant to commemorate the original All-Alaska Sweepstakes Race and to memorialize Seppala himself.

In 1926, in honor of his dogs' participation in the rescue effort, Seppala and his dogs toured the Lower Forty-Eight. The tour included a ten-day stint at Madison Square Garden, where his lead dog, Togo, received an honorary gold medal.

Arthur T. Walden and his dog, Chinook.
PHOTO COURTESY OF PERRY GREENE KENNEL HISTORIC COLLECTION

While in New England, Seppala ran his team in a race in Poland Springs, Maine, where participants and spectators once again scoffed at the huskies' size compared to that of the larger New England dogs, including Walden's Chinooks. This time, the huskies took first place. Two weeks later, the team entered and won a more prestigious race in Laconia, New Hampshire. These races piqued New Englanders' interest in huskies, and Seppala worked with a breeder in Poland Springs to establish a stock of Siberians in the region.

Mushing communities sprouted up in many of the northern states in a similar way. Prospectors returning from the Arctic brought back dogs or a plan to breed dogs for mushing. Races attracted the press and increased the sport's visibility. The 1920s and 1930s were the golden age of mushing, which became

PHOTO BY RICK FROST

Tenley Meara's team, one of many, during a race in Sandwich Notch, New Hampshire.

one of North America's fastest-growing sports. The 1932 Olympic Games in Lake Placid, New York, even featured demonstration races. But World War II marked a slowdown, as many breeders and mushers donated their dogs to the war effort. The animals would serve in Arctic search and rescue operations and for scouting and communication in the Battle of the Bulge.

Mushing for sport picked up again after the war, but with less momentum. There was less interest in the sport outside the established breeding and mushing communities. Today, sled dog organizations across the northern states support sled dog breeding and local races. Particularly active groups exist in Oregon, Idaho, Minnesota, the Tug Hill Plateau of upstate New York, and throughout New England. These organizations support weekly events, which include sprint and distance races for teams of every size and mushers of every age. Technology has improved sleds, making them lighter and less expensive. Skijoring—mushing on skis with only one-to-three dogs—has gained popularity over the past two decades. These innovations have made it easier for people to practice mushing as a recreational sport.

Still, mushing is in no way a casual sport. It takes time and resources to feed and transport dogs; maintain sleds, harnesses, and trucks; and get to regional races hundreds of miles apart. Race purses are often too small to reimburse even the winning team for its weekend expenses. Participating mushers are intensely dedicated to a way of life that leaves little room for other activities. The rest of us can enjoy the sport from the sidelines. We can attend races to get a taste of the colorful world of dog sledding, and we can even enjoy guided rides offered by mushers who are expanding their operations to take advantage of the tourist industry.

IN MAINE'S 100-MILE-WILDERNESS COMMUNITIES, THE APPALACHIAN Mountain Club is joining local sporting clubs, businesses, and landowners as they work to reinvigorate the economy. The region's logging and railroad booms are long over, and the economy now depends largely on tourism—fishing in the summer, hunting in the fall, and snowmobiling in the winter. Recently, the communities have begun developing activities to encourage ecotourism. While motorized snow sports have helped maintain a tourist base, residents hope that

Player and Savick are two of Tenley Meara's playful Alaskan huskies.

a focus on nonmotorized sports will help bring additional tourists to the area.* That is how the idea of a 100-Mile Wilderness Sled Dog Race was born.

The inaugural race took off on a bright day in February 2005 as part of Greenville's SnoFest, a two-week "celebration of winter sports." Connecting the towns of Greenville and Brownville Junction, the wilderness course traverses conservation lands. But the connection wasn't only via trail. Planning and implementing this event brought community members and a wide variety of interest groups together in a new spirit of cooperation, most notably between motorized and nonmotorized winter sports enthusiasts. The snowmobile clubs helped groom the trails and keep the passage clear for the dog teams; local mushing clubs helped coordinate schedules with other regional races; and students volunteered to help handle the dogs. Ham radio enthusiasts arranged communication between course checkpoints and area businesses stayed open for spectators. Eleven teams from Quebec, Vermont, New Hampshire, and Maine converged on the region and helped open up a new era of cooperation and progress.

MIDDAY IN THE TOWN OF BROWNVILLE JUNCTION, THE DOG TEAMS converge at the halfway point and take respite in the plowed parking area near the local grocery store and American Legion center. After my glimpse of the first team to pass the Crystal Lake checkpoint near the Katahdin Iron Works gate earlier that day, I moved to where I could see the teams taking a sharp corner, and I learned to appreciate not only the small dogs' stamina and precision, but their utter focus on the race itself.

Watching the mushers struggle to bed down the dogs in soft hay for some well-deserved rest, it is clear how much these animals love running. Many of them strain against the harnesses, hoping to break free and start the run back to the trail. Frozen bricks of fish and other treats finally convince them to stick around. As they relax, a local veterinarian checks their vitals and paws, and their mushers apply lotion to their pads and blankets to their backs.

There are two teams of what I think of as huskies, but which I learn are, more specifically, Siberian huskies. The rest of the dogs appear to be mixed

---

*See *Appalachia: Summer/Fall 2005* for information about the Appalachian Mountain Club's Maine Woods Initiative, which seeks to conserve lands in the 100-Mile Wilderness region and support the local economy by promoting nature-based recreation and tourism.

Sled dog with a snowy nose.

breeds—shepherd, collie, greyhound. But as I wander along the rope barrier protecting the resting teams from overeager fans, I chat with the mushers and learn that these seeming mutts are in fact Alaskan huskies. They are indeed larger than Siberians but still smaller and more wiry than what I had expected. My image of them, I finally realized, had been based on the Jack London stories about freight-pulling dogs, which are really malamutes and Samoyeds.

After an afternoon of rest, the teams start off to complete the second half of the race, the return to Greenville over miles of woods and snow. Volunteers help handle the dogs who, in their excitement to return to the trail, sometimes tangle their harnesses. As they are readied to return to the race, they yelp with abandon. But once the countdown gets to "TWO," the handlers step away and the mushers step onto the sleds, and the dogs get down to the business of running.*

---

*That day, the winning team belonged to musher André Longchamps from Port Rouge, Québec. His team of twelve huskies made the 100-mile trek in 8 hours, 56 minutes, arriving in Greenville at 8:48. Race day trail conditions were "punchy," due to a recent blizzard, which produced 22 inches of snow; temperatures ranged from 10 degrees to 32 degrees, without wind chill.

New England's cold winter temperatures and ample snowfall make for enjoyable times on the trail for dogs and musher alike. On this day, in northern Vermont, the temperature barely made it above zero degrees.

Though the dogs are gone, the crowd remains. As the camera crew from a local TV station packs up, journalists make their rounds, and some children pick up a snowball fight, while others head over to the American Legion for dinner. As a new event for the region's mushers, the race means welcome expansion for the sport. The enthusiastic crowds and positive attention also mean that the new race is a triumph for this community and a model for regional interdependence and cooperation.

THE 2006 100-MILE WILDERNESS SLED DOG RACE WILL RUN ON FEBRUARY 11th and will again be organized and supported by the towns of Greenville, Brownville, and Brownville Junction, the Appalachian Mountain Club, Moosehead Riders Snowmobile Club, Natural Resource Education Center, Northwoods Healthy Communities, and the Greenville American Legion. (At press time, additional sponsors were being solicited.)

For more information, including race times, volunteering opportunities, and points from which to view the race, go to www.trcmaine.org/sledrace. For information about lodging in the area and more, see www.greenvilleme. com, www.mooseheadlake.org, www.trcmaine.org. You may also contact Amy Dugan of Mountain Ridge at info@mtnridge.com.

For more information about Northeastern Sled Dog Clubs and Races, go to:
- New England Sled Dog Club at www.nesdc.org
- The Downeast Sled Dog Club, Inc. at www.desdc.org
- The Maine Highlands Sled Dog Club at www.critterwoods.com/ sleddogclub.htm
- The Yankee Siberian Husky Club, Inc. at www.yshc.org

For more information about Guided Dog Sledding Opportunities in New Hampshire and Maine, go to:
- Appalachian Mountain Club Outdoor Adventures at www.outdoors.org/education
- Mountain Ridge at www.mtnridge.com
- Mahoosuc Guide Service at www.mahoosuc.com
- Bear River Mushing at bearrivermushing.tripod.com
- Morning Crescent at www.sledpets.com
- Song in the Woods at www.songinthewoods.com
- Tugline Kennels at www.mushnh.com

For other regions, see www.dogsledrides.com.

SARAH JANE SHANGRAW served as editor-in-chief of AMC Books from 2003–2005.

Avalanche Training on Alaska's Slopes

Hard Lessons from Arctic Snow

By Alys Culhane

M AKE SURE YOUR PROBE LINE IS STRAIGHT," YELLED ALASKA Avalanche School instructor Kip Melling. As if on cue, we thrust our poles into the snow pack, aligned our feet, stood palm to palm, and waited for our next order.

"Go ahead, John, you're in charge," Melling said.

"Probe left, probe center, probe right, move forward," shouted seventeen-year-old line leader John Hundley.

"Keep moving in lockstep," Melling urged.

"Hey," Alaska State Park employee Robin Kling yelled. "There's something soft and squishy here."

We circled Kling, and with probes in hand, poked gingerly at the soft snow. Something soft and squishy turned out to be Melling's backpack. I glanced at our instructor, who smiled broadly. But the event caused me to come to a potentially life-saving realization. Probe rescues are tedious, time-consuming, and involve much more room for error than do beacon rescues. It would be in my best interest to purchase an avalanche beacon, and to be vigilant about using it. I'd do a beacon check, and strap the device under my coat before stepping out of the parking lot. I'd also insist that my traveling companions do the same.

"Okay, let's get back to work," Melling said.

I live in Palmer, Alaska, near Anchorage, home of the Alaska Avalanche School (AAS). In preparation for the AAS's Level 1 Backcountry Avalanche Hazard Evaluation and Rescue course, I had taken a preclass quiz, which should have alerted me to just how comprehensive this course would be. Based at the Hatcher Pass Visitor's Center in the Talkeetna Mountains, the class included much more than rescue-related material. By the end of the three-day course, I would acquire the hands-on skills to recognize and evaluate potential avalanche hazards, and I would practice terrain analysis, snow stability evaluation, decision-making, safe travel procedures, and backcountry route selection.

After doing three more role-playing sessions, our group (dubbed the Depth Hoars) returned to the interior of the Visitor's Center, where we again joined the Spatial Dendrites, the Hard Slabs, and the Sastrugi Warriors.

My 24 classmates, who ranged in age from 16 to 55, came from all walks of life. Four Palmer area high school students, two Fairbanks-based engineers, and ten members of the FBI participated in the late-January class. I was

Opposite: Prod line work is tedious, time consuming, and laborious. Left to right: Alys Culhane, Robin Kling, Bryan Quimby, and John Hundley. PHOTO BY PETE PRAETORIUS

Bryan and Alys look on as Nancy Pfieffer records the test pit data into her log book.

PHOTO BY PETE PRAETORIUS

one of three female enrollees. We all had to meet the course prerequisites, which included being able to remain outside in foul weather and to ski or snowshoe up and downhill in variable terrain and changing snow conditions. When we introduced ourselves to each other at 8 A.M., I mentioned that a day trip to Hatcher Pass with one of the course instructors had led me to realize that I should take the course before embarking on any long trips.

The four instructors did not disappoint. Eagle River resident Melling, Palmer resident Nancy Pfeiffer, Eagle River resident Blaine Smith, and guest instructor Eric White (who lives and works in Mount Shasta, California) assisted us in developing what AAS founder Doug Fesler called our "avalanche eyeballs." All expert backcountry skiers and trained avalanche educators and forecasters, they take their jobs seriously.

Melling, Pfeiffer, and Smith are long-time employees of AAS, a nonprofit organization that is an offshoot of the Alaska Mountain Safety Center. The school's courses were originally designed and taught by Anchorage residents and avalanche experts Fesler and Jill Fredston, who founded the center in 1977. Since its inception, the AAS has led the country in avalanche education. To prepare for my course, I had I read Fesler and Fredston's *Snow Sense*.

Because the instructors believe people learn best by doing, they emphasize hands-on training. But current instructors have modified that approach by putting together a series of PowerPoint presentations that enable students to see a wide variety of snowpacks and terrain types in a short amount of time.

I took notes as our instructors talked about the conditions that lent themselves to avalanche formation: "Terrain-related causes of avalanches include steep slopes; weather-related causes include strong winds, new snow, and temperature fluctuations; and snowpack-related causes include more cohesive layers, which form slabs over weaker layers."

On Day Two, we followed our instructors out into the field and collected the data that we'd later use in compiling a group forecast. Pfeiffer led the Depth Hoars. We skied and snowshoed in the direction of Friendship Pass, stopping frequently to observe the snow type, the wind speed, the amount of drift — all variables that are central to assessing stability or instability.

We also practiced using our inclinometers, plastic, credit-card-size devices with lead weights attached to fishing line. I repeatedly checked the area slope angles, looking for "prime time" or dangerous angles, which are between 30 and 45 degrees.

Midday, Pfeiffer asked some young members of our group to dig three snow pits. Cutting into the layers exposed the season's snowpack and allowed us to conduct stratigraphy, resistance, hardness, compression, and finally, shear block tests. I peered over her shoulder as Pfeiffer recorded our initial data in her snow pit book. She explained to me that her written seasonal findings enable her to determine if area snowpacks are getting stronger or weaker.

We further tested stability with the Rutschblock and Banzai Jump Tests. The former is used to test the snow's strength in response to the weight of one person, and the latter to test strength in response to the weight of several people. During the Rutschblock test, the snowpack failed to budge when Harlon Guthrie repeatedly jumped on it, indicating that it was very stable. During the Banzai Jump Test, I watched, chagrined, as Pfeiffer, Guthrie, Hundley (the line leader from the probing exercise), and Bryan Quimby linked their arms, flexed their knees, and applied considerable force to the snowpack. It held. Pfeiffer then drew an imaginary line across the upper one-third of the pack.

"Now," she said, "on the count of three, I want you to do a coordinated jump. And aim for this line," she said, pointing to it with the tip of her blue ski boot. The four yelled and jumped hard, three times. The top layers of the block broke off at the place where they'd predicted it would. Both jump tests confirmed what the less physical tests had indicated — that the snowpack layer was stable. Before leaving the pit area, we filled it back in as a courtesy to other hikers.

The second day's field lesson culminated with an hour-long lesson on back-country travel safety. Individually, we hiked to the base of Friendship Pass, maintaining an equal amount of distance between us. Beforehand, Pfeiffer had explained that traveling one at a time reduces the likelihood of a mass burial. Furthermore, the other hikers are in a better position to assist if someone runs into trouble.

Later in the day, all groups, under Pfeiffer's direction, compiled a collective group weather forecast, which indicated that conditions for backcountry travel in the immediate Hatcher Pass area were favorable.

Although we all thought otherwise, the class day wasn't over. One instructor, Smith, picked two "assistants" from among us, then poured sugar, flour, and potato flakes into their cupped hands. The grinning students sifted the individual materials onto a flat board studded with fake rocks and trees. As Smith raised the board, another assistant pulled his inclinometer from his pocket and measured slope angles. The unstable layers slid to the bottom of the board, burying the "town" below. After the laughter died down, an instructor pointed out that what remained on the board were the characteristic components of an avalanche—the crown, or uppermost portion; the flanks, or sides; the bed surface; and the debris pile.

Day Three's class included a backcountry trek, and the morning's lectures centered around human factors and route selection. As his voice rose and fell, Smith stressed the importance of traveling with knowledgeable group members, keeping the lines of communication open, working as a team, and paying close attention to what you observe as you go.

The morning proceeded with a brief lesson in how to read a topographical map and a talk on the importance of essential gear. From his pack, Smith extracted a blue ensolite foam pad (used to hold broken limbs in place), a voluminous red nylon bivy sack (used to provide shelter and warmth to hypo-thermic individuals), and a handsaw (used to cut pit layers and wood for shelter and fires).

On our way to our destination, Murphy Lake, we examined the remains of a slab avalanche that had occurred earlier that month. From where we were standing, we could make out the crown, flanks, and debris pile. Inclinometers in hand, we measured the slope angle and speculated about the possibility of another avalanche. Much to my relief, Smith said that based on given terrain, weather, and snow pack information, another avalanche in this particular area would be an anomalous occurrence. Our last task involved doing an informal stability analysis of the crown of the earlier avalanche.

Upon returning to the lodge, Pfeiffer explained that we were now going to determine what course of action to take on an imaginary backcountry trip. She presented us with cards, each of which contained specific information on terrain, snow pack, weather, and human factors. We were instructed to give each variable a rating, and based on our findings, to determine if our trip should proceed. Our group's trip was initially looking like a go: visibility was excellent, temperatures had been stable, the wind was calm, and the slope angle in the terrain we'd be traveling in was 26 degrees, below the danger level. But there was one red flag: the snowpack consisted of an unstable, 6-inch surface layer.

Should we go or wait? The twenty-minute debate was lively.

We concluded that since our slope angle was below avalanche range, we could proceed. But, we agreed, we'd need to be extremely careful in selecting and following our route. At that point, I realized I was more able to make educated decisions about the pros and cons of embarking on backcountry travel. I was certainly more avalanche savvy. But I was also more respectful of the snow—and mindful of the need to look for and heed every one of its signals.

ALYS CULHANE, a former resident of Palmer, Alaska, currently lives in Butte, Montana, where she's putting the finishing touches on *Headwinds: The Memoirs of a Cross-Country Bicyclist*. Culhane is also preparing to ride horseback from Canada to Mexico on the Continental Divide Bicycle Trail. Her essay, "Reading Ice," appeared in the Winter 2004/2005 issue of *Appalachia*.

A Light in Winter Woods

By Douglas Haynes

T HE WOODS STARTLED ME. IT WAS A TYPICAL WINTER AFTERNOON in Vermont's Northeast Kingdom: snowflakes meandering down from a heavy pall of clouds. I was snowshoeing over an old logging road up out of the valley where I live, on my way to a waterfall that tumbles over a cliff face from a beaver pond perched above it. Hemlocks and cedars tunneled me in, the contrast between their branches and the snow creating an Ansel Adams–like landscape of crisp blacks and whites. The stillness added to my sense that I was walking through a picture. No croaks from the usual ravens. Not even the chatter of chickadees.

For the first time in four days the temperature had crested zero, and I had been inside too long. I didn't expect to see much in the dull weather, though: visibility was limited to a quarter mile or so, and it had been snowing long enough to obscure any fresh animal tracks. The kind of day that has often caused me to resent winter for what I've perceived as its lack of natural variety.

When I reached the falls, I was grateful for the rush of water, though the stream was hidden beneath a gray layer of ice. More than a trickle, not quite a roar. The company of sound on an afternoon so quiet was almost oppressive. And then it started: an electric glow hovered over the slope by the falls like the orange patina of city lights on a low, overcast sky at night. I looked to the west to see if the sun might be peeking through the clouds as it sometimes does just before setting. But there wasn't the slightest break in the clouds above the western rim of the valley. And no city could cast its lights so close to the ground. The underbrush continued to glow, a warm being amidst the lifeless woods.

Having grown up in rolling, open country cropped with corn and soybeans, I am not yet accustomed to the constantly changing perspectives that come with walking the steep, wooded slopes of northern Vermont. After living here two years, I still feel as if my eyes have to be reinvented every day to discern the subtleties of the forest close at hand and the shifting forms of the middle distance. I only need to go a few hundred yards from my house in any direction to see entirely different prospects: mountains hide or appear, a lake glistens or goes completely black.

Guessing that a new perspective might unravel the mystery of the glowing, I shuffled 10 feet up the path past the falls. As I moved, the blurry color ebbed into the distinct, bronze leaves of a cluster of young beech trees. I felt silly. From where I stood before, the leaves were undifferentiated, just a brightness suspended in the otherwise darkening woods. Once I knew the

Opposite: Winter forest scene near Tuckerman Ravine. PHOTO BY JERRY AND MARCY MONKMAN

Snow shadows on a northern hardwood forest.

source of that color, I could no longer see it as a presence. The enigma of the whole had dissolved into knowable parts.

But that only strengthened the significance of the glowing I saw before. I have never seen the winter woods here the same way again. That afternoon, when the land seemed spiritless and uniform, the beeches' propensity for holding their leaves through the coldest days of the year became an emblem of winter's aesthetic possibilities. And I realized that we all have our beeches: unexpected visions of the land that awake us to ways of becoming more at home in our places. We shouldn't feel ashamed if our eyes are untrained; their tricks can remind us that — even in the deepest throes of winter — the land is a reservoir of warm surprises. The longer I live in these woods, the more my senses evolve with them. The more I expect to be startled again.

Douglas Haynes is a poet, freelance writer, and translator, whose work has appeared in *Orion Online*, *Birding*, and many other publications. Currently in exile from Vermont's Northeast Kingdom, he lives in Lebanon, New Hampshire.

the clouds

the glacier of air above
settles,
      whitens,
           disintegrates,
burns
to a solar dust
      storm,
turns bedsheets of thunder,
  a stray is a lost loved one following you,
routing of birdsong, transfigurations gentler
   than mist on the climber, distant
  bolts, sunny landscape accents, models for clay,
foam-running offings,
               water shaping air
air shaping water

—Francis Blessington

Francis Blessington has published two books of poems: *Wolf Howl* (BkMk Press, University of Missouri-KC, 2000) and *Lantskip* (William Bauhan, 1987). He has also published many essays and short stories. His latest book is a novel, *The Last Witch of Dogtown* (Curious Traveler Press, 2001).

The Fascinating Life of Marion Davis

Cobuilder of the Wapack Trail and Pioneer Lodge Owner

By Christine Woodside

PHOTO COURTESY OF BRUCE C. BUCK

On July 29, 1993, an electrical storm ignited a vacant house on Routes 123/124 in New Ipswich, New Hampshire, leaving it a shell of blackened siding reaching toward the sky. Arsonists had previously vandalized the building, but its final destruction was a shock. This empty house had once been the Wapack Lodge, the former home of Marion Buck Robbins Davis, who hosted hikers and skiers there between 1925 and 1958 while they were traversing the 21-mile Wapack Trail. The Wapack was the first interstate hiking path of the twentieth century, and Davis may well have been the first female trail builder, maintainer, and hiking lodge caretaker.

Neighbor Al Jenks, who had bought land from Marion many years before, told a newspaper reporter after the fire, "My loss is thinking about her and missing her. Marion was the Wapack Lodge."

In a way, too, Davis was the Wapack Trail. Some of the guests stayed for days or weeks on end to enjoy her home cooking. Not to mention her company. This most unusual woman had scouted the trail in the early 1920s with Frank Robbins (whom she later married). She named the trail, joining the "Wa" from its starting point, Mount Watatic in Ashburnham, Massachusetts, with the "Pack" of its end point, North Pack Monadnock in Greenfield, New Hampshire. Davis also chose the triangular-shaped blazes as a symbol of friendship.

The 1993 lodge fire, which occurred seven years after Davis's death, resulted in more than the loss of the building. It was also the destruction of Davis's brilliant project, which made hiking and skiing convenient for city people. It would be fair to suggest that in the lodge's busiest seasons, Davis's hospitality drew people to the trail as much as the open ridges, pine forests, and quiet ponds did.

Marion and Frank ran the lodge starting in 1925, when the Appalachian Trail was still mostly a concept. In fact, one frequent guest at the lodge was Benton MacKaye, the landscape architect who had conceived the idea of the Appalachian Trail. For a few Octobers running, MacKaye stayed at the Wapack Lodge for two weeks at a time.

These were the early years of the backcountry trail movement that grabbed the northeastern United States in the 1920s and 1930s. So many adventurers were traversing the low ridges between Mount Watatic and North Pack

Marion, second from the left, on the summit of one of the Wapack mountains. The woman standing on the left is Ruth Porter. She is believed to be Marion's daughter. At far right is Marion's sister, Alice.

Zenafon Allen on the porch of Wapack Lodge, 1925.

Monadnock that, on one February weekend, the Peterborough Transcript reported that there was no room left to park at the trail crossings and that more than 1,000 people were on the trail. Hikers and skiers could break up the trip—and avoid having to get off the trail at the end of a long day—by staying at the trailside lodge, which stood at roughly the halfway point. Davis served fresh meat, homegrown vegetables, and homemade baked goods to hundreds of hikers each season.

Davis's trailside hospitality might suggest a method of maintaining interest today in the many quiet trails of the Northeast, like the Wapack. Fewer hikers enjoy the full lengths of these trails today, because camping areas and trailside lodges are rare. Hikers who yearn to follow a pilgrimage from Point A to Point B must often patch together section hikes, asking relatives or friends to pick them up or doubling back over the same terrain. Today on the Wapack, Al Jenks rents out lean-tos north of the summit of Barrett Mountain on his Windblown Ski Touring Center land, providing the only opportunity to stay overnight.

From the City to the Farm

The story of Marion Davis's long life has never been told completely. She was born Marion Buck in Fitchburg, Massachusetts, on February 8, 1894, in a house her carpenter father built. She was the second of six children. When she was young, the family moved to North Carolina to follow her father's building projects. A year and a half later, they returned to Massachusetts. "Dad had lost so much money on that job in North Carolina that we had to sell the little cottage, and we went back into the tenement house, only in the upstairs instead of the middle tenement," Davis recalled on a tape of her memories made in the 1980s, near the end of her life.

Despite her father's money troubles, Marion and her brothers and sisters seemed to enjoy an ordinary and happy childhood. Nothing about her early life suggested the unusually independent woman she would become. She played outside, picked blueberries, went to church and school, and at thirteen, helped organize a sewing club, the Zig-Zag Club. That year, 1907, they all moved briefly to Panama, where her father constructed housing for the Panama Canal builders. Marion recalled having to cut up 4-foot log lengths for cooking. "The man who delivered the wood said, 'Do you have to cut this up?' and I said, 'Yes.' He said, 'Well, I'll give you a few pointers.'"

During her early teen years back in Fitchburg, Marion wanted to study drawing, but her mother objected. She soon left school and started working for a neighbor, who briefly fired her in a dispute over whether the stair risers were clean. That summer, she spent two weeks on a farm in Rindge, New Hampshire, where her mother had grown up. The couple who ran the farm, the Robbinses, had no children and took in orphans. They had never formally adopted Marion's mother, Helen, but they considered her their daughter. When life got awkward for eighteen-year-old Marion at home, her mother's adoptive family welcomed her to the farm. It was a life-altering trip from which she never returned.

"There was more or less friction between Mother and me and I was saucy to her one time," Marion recounts on the tape. "She gave me three days to apologize or to move out." By one account, she had scratches from her altercation. She asked advice of her employer, a dentist in town, and he advised her to go to the farm if she could. "So I left home," Marion said. "November 19, 1912, to go to the farm. I had a good nervous breakdown."

At the farm she met Frank Robbins, her mother's half-brother by adoption. Frank's mother was one of the adopted children, and his father was the farm owner. By the time Marion met him he was in his thirties and had a wife, Mabel.

On the farm, Marion learned to ride horses and wagons and to move cattle from Groton, Massachusetts, to pastures in Rindge. She milked cows; delivered milk; raised vegetables, corn, and other grains; and learned about running a grist mill. She also helped to clear an area around a well, cutting down her first pine tree solo, slicing her leg in the process. But she loved the outdoor life.

Within two years, she had fallen in love with Frank and become pregnant. The scandal so jarred her family that the daughter Marion gave birth to in 1914, Ruth, was not permitted to identify her true mother in public. It seems that few people knew that Marion had a daughter. Even when newspapers wrote about the trail or the lodge, the reporters referred to Frank either as Marion's uncle or her husband. Frank remained married to Mabel but spent much time with Marion. It seems that Marion had a hand in raising her daughter, although she never discussed it publicly.

The Wapack Trail Is Born

Marion and Frank were doing some haying on the low ridges of New Ipswich in the summer of 1922 when the Wapack Trail first entered their consciousness. Allen Chamberlain, a newspaperman from Boston who was living in nearby Jaffrey that year, stopped up to see them. With him was Albert Annett, a box factory owner in Jaffrey. Annett told Frank and Marion that he wanted their help scouting a hiking trail on the ridge, where Frank owned 1,200 acres. Frank and Marion were enthusiastic.

"Working mainly on Sundays, when farm chores were less pressing, they brushed out the trail in approximately four months, marking it at regular intervals with a white triangle, the symbol of friendship," wrote a nephew, David Dillon, in an unpublished biography of Davis. At the urging of Arthur Comey, a Boston city planner and ardent outdoorsman, they also cut out a ski trail on the protected slopes so that, by the end of 1923, the Wapack was open year-round."

The hiking and skiing must have been spectacular. The low ridges were mostly open then because of seasonal cattle grazing, and the views were wonderful, showing Mount Monadnock and beyond. The openness of these ridges remains in a few places today. The elevation is in the 2,000- to 3,000-foot range.

By 1924, Marion and Frank were building a hikers' lodge over an old cellar-hole on Routes 123/124, at the edge of the trail. It augmented their farming

Frank and Marion at the Wapack Lodge, winter 1924.

income and gave hikers a place to stay.

Benton MacKaye could well have been describing his experience of Marion's trailside hospitality when he outlined his concept of "wilderness ways" in the magazine *Landscape Architecture* in 1929. He described the need for shorter trails as week-end destinations. "The wilderness way should follow the stretches of wild country," he wrote. "The object of the wilderness way is to provide a *living ground*, not merely a playground, nor a visiting ground: it is to provide a leisure place for leisure time; the primeval environment is our primary home. The time for this particular kind of home-going is provided in our week-ends and in our vacation periods. But how about the *place*? The place, for one thing, must be near at hand, within quick and inexpensive access from the centers of population."

MacKaye listed two trails in his article, the Wapack and the adjacent 22-mile-long Sprague Trail from Mount Wachusett to Mount Watatic, as part of a "rim" of paths near Boston. He also promoted trailside camping, and although he did not talk about an actual building like the Wapack Lodge, some of what he said about remaining on the trail rather than having to go home at night could easily have come out of his repeated and lengthy experiences on the Wapack.

"To really live in a place one must be enabled to stay over night," MacKaye wrote. "This requires an abode — for our purposes it requires a primeval abode,

Frank and Marion on their wedding day.

because we are seeking a primeval environment: it requires a camping place (or a series thereof) suitable equipped and conveniently located. To really live in a place one must also be enabled to travel in it." He said the hiking, canoeing, and horseback riding would provide an occupation within the wilderness, rather than going in circles. "Men walking in a loop will not suffice; the desire is linear and not round, tangential and not circular; it is to proceed from one scene and sphere into another, to have at our service the full view of the continent even if we use but a particle: in short, to widen our horizon."

Life in the Landscape

One of the fascinating traits of Marion Davis was that her horizon was so narrow—the farmlands and the lodge—and yet so satisfying to her. She was no hermit, though. Everyone who knew Davis has said she was delightful and a great storyteller. Clearly, she loved company. Many who visited her in her later years got to hear her stories of Wapack Lodge guests and read through the lists of names in her guestbooks.

She also was a highly skilled farmer who understood the woods and the weather. For several years she sent telegrams with weather conditions to the Appalachian Mountain Club. So efficient was Davis at timber splitting that in 1935, she won a woman's wood-chopping contest. A winter carnival had come to nearby Wilton. The organizers heard about Davis from some locals, and they came tramping through the woods near the Wapack Lodge to ask her if she would enter the women's division.

"I was down by the ice pond trimming out a tree that Frank had cut down, when I heard a voice behind me say, 'Good! That's just the way we hoped we'd find you,'" Marion remembered in her unpublished biography. "I refused, not wanting to make a public fool of myself, but Frank spoke up and agreed for me on the spot. He spent three hours grinding my axe, and then we set off, me in coontail felt boots and all." She made three cuts in a 12-inch hardwood log in five minutes, thirteen seconds. Her trophy proclaimed her the international woman's woodchopping champion. She had to decline the dinner invitation that came with the prize, though; there were guests at the lodge.

By that time, the lodge had become the center of Marion's life. She had been living there from the time it opened, while Frank traveled back and forth between the lodge in New Ipswich and the farmhouse in Rindge, where his wife Mabel lived until her death in 1945. Frank and Marion were free to marry then, but Frank insisted on a one-year wait. They married at last in 1946, and the new Mr. and Mrs. Robbins went on a northern honeymoon to places like Niagara Falls. Soon after, Frank contracted bone cancer, which claimed his life in 1947.

After Frank's death, Marion's niece, Constance Buck Hall of Fitchburg,

Marion at the dedication of the Marion Davis Trail, 1986.

said that the men in the area might well have lined up to marry Marion, because she was so sweet and fun to be around. Marion did marry for a second time, to another farmer named Lawrence Davis. The two of them ran the lodge until 1958, the year they registered their last guest. Lawrence became ill and died soon after. But while they continued to live there, Marion took a job as a cook in the nearby schools. Jenks recalled that discipline problems were sent to her, and that the kids would follow her around the kitchen.

In later years, after Lawrence's death, Marion lived across the street from the lodge in a trailer. She put up a sign, "Trail Information," and continued to hand out maps until her final illness in the mid-1980s.

Friends of the Wapack Trail

In 1980, a local group formed to care for the Wapack. These Friends of the Wapack Trail worked with landowners to protect the trail and took over maintenance work from the AMC's Worcester chapter. In 1986, a few months before Marion's death, the Friends rededicated an alternate trail to the summit of Pack Monadnock, naming it the Marion Davis Trail. She told a friend that she would have rather seen it named for Frank Robbins. For the dedication ceremony that September 29, Marion revealed to the public for the first time that she had not only a daughter, but a granddaughter, a great-granddaughter, and a great-great-grandson. All of them came to the ceremony and posed with Marion for the Monadnock Ledger.

Constance Buck Hall believes that the lodge was a key element in the Wapack Trail's success and a very important part of Marion's life. In her taped memoir, Marion said, "Well, having a trail was the incentive for having a place to put folks up overnight. For years, my sister, Alice, had been at me to go in with her on a tearoom business somewhere."

Like Benton MacKaye, Marion Davis understood that in order to maintain a public trail, there must be people living near it who love it and who want to get to it. She was truly a pioneer, independent and hardy, and a committed conservationist in a time when most women were still wearing white gloves.

CHRISTINE WOODSIDE is a writer who lives in Deep River, a hiker who discovered the Wapack Trail in August 2004, and, beginning in December, will be the new Editor-in-Chief of *Appalachia*.

On the Appalachian Trail, above Delaware Water Gap

Up on the ridge the October sun still sifts
down enough warmth that a few blueberry

come into second bloom. Early morning
and quiet: I've no reason not to stop, to sit.

The white bells of the blossoms look like souls,
auburn leaves like blood that must spill

if the soul is to depart. At this hour
the grasses wet my legs, spider webs

outlined by dew, by the blue above their nests.
In the distance two nuclear reactors send

steam into the air: ghosts of uranium,
plutonium, of water turned against itself.

Two hawks and four vultures have surfaced
while I've sat here. They ride the updrafts

that rise along the cliff face. They see a world
that will come long after these petals fall.

—*Todd Davis*

TODD DAVIS teaches English and Environmental Studies at Penn State Altoona. His first collection of poetry, *Ripe*, appeared in 2002. His new work is in recent or forthcoming issues of *The North American Review*, *Midwest Quarterly*, *Flyway*, and *Blueline*.

On Snowy, Uphill Trails with a Four-Legged Hiking Legend

By Steven D. Smith

D URING THE PAST SEVERAL WINTERS, HIKERS IN THE HIGH PEAKS of New Hampshire's White Mountains have been startled by what looked like a small bear ambling down the trail. But that was no sleepwalking bruin; that was "Brutus," a 160-pound Newfoundland who has become a canine legend on the winter trails.

Accompanied by his owner, Kevin Rooney, 57, formerly of Williamstown, Vermont, and a merry band of fellow hikers, Brutus (or "Mr. B," as he is sometimes affectionately called) has climbed all forty-eight of New Hampshire's 4,000-foot peaks in winter. Not once, but twice.

In this game, under rules established by the AMC's 4,000-Footer Committee, the summits must be climbed during calendar winter, typically December 22 to March 20. This involves twenty-five- to thirty-day hikes, covering more than 200 miles of steep terrain, including the barren, wind-blasted crests of Mount Washington and its Presidential Range neighbors. Slightly more than 300 human hikers have achieved this milestone, compared to nearly 8,000 who have climbed the peaks in the warmer months, but Brutus is the first dog to earn the coveted winter patch.

The challenges of the high summits in winter—snow, cold, ice, wind, and wildly changeable weather—keep most sensible hikers, human or canine, curled up in front of the fireplace. But this is the time of year when Brutus, with his luxuriant coat of black fur, thrives on the trail.

"Mr. B loves the snow," said Rooney, a genial man who has taught numerous winter hiking workshops for the AMC. "It's a lot more comfortable for him than hiking in the heat of summer."

Brutus, who turned five this December, boasts a noble lineage. His breed is noted for its strong physique and sweet disposition. Both his parents were Canadian dog show champions, and his full registered name is "Brutus the Mighty King." He began hiking soon after Rooney and his wife acquired him, ascending Vermont's Camel's Hump in October 2001. A week later, Brutus and Rooney hiked the rugged 9-mile loop over Mounts Lincoln and Lafayette in Franconia Notch. Though Mr. B struggled a bit that day, Rooney said, "I could tell he was very strong, and cold, windy, snowy conditions with rime ice didn't faze him at all."

Within a year, Brutus had polished off his "all-season" list of New Hampshire 4,000-footers. According to an AMC tradition dating back to the 1960s,

Opposite: Brutus with Scot Holt on the shoulder of Mt. Clay on the Jewell Trail.
PHOTO BY KEVIN ROONEY

PHOTO BY KEVIN ROONEY

Brutus joins Kevin Rooney, Jeff Kuehl, and Jim Durning on the roof of the Lakes Hut.

canine climbers receive formal recognition for their accomplishments. So the following spring, Brutus and Rooney attended the annual awards dinner held in Stratham, New Hampshire, by the 4,000-Footer Committee. The 200 as-sembled peakbaggers clapped and whistled while Brutus paraded down the aisle for the patch and congratulatory pawshake.

Brutus began his winter climbs of the forty-eight peaks just after he fin-ished his all-season climbs. On a trek to Wildcat Mountain in January 2003, a playful Brutus delighted his human companions by sliding down a ski trail on his side. During the winter of 2003–04, Brutus rambled through the rest of his winter list, as Rooney posted reports of their trips on the popular hikers' website, www.viewsfromthetop.com. A small cadre of devoted winter hikers accompanied the pair on most of their treks. Many others followed the gentle giant's exploits on the Web.

On January 18, 2004, Brutus tagged winter summit number forty-eight atop Mount Pierce in the Presidential Range. He was rewarded with a spe-cial treat of steak tips, carried to the summit by fellow peakbagger Cathy Goodwin. That spring, Mr. B made an encore appearance at the 4,000-footer awards event, where he received a whooping round of applause.

The following summer, Rooney mapped out a plan for climbing all of the peaks in a single calendar winter. This had first been done by Cathy Goodwin, Cindy DiSanto, and Steven Martin in the winter of 1994–5 and had since been replicated by only a handful of two-legged hikers.

During the winter of 2004–5, the adventures of "Kevin, Brutus & Friends" appeared on the web several times each week. Early in the season, a series of thaws and freezes encased the trails in ice, creating hazardous conditions. Rooney was prepared for nearly every eventuality, however. For the steep descent of the Blueberry Ledge Trail off Mount Whiteface, he brought along a harness and rope to lower Brutus over the trickiest ledges.

"While he wasn't crazy about it at first, by the end of the third pitch he had it figured out, and the fourth went rather smoothly," wrote Rooney in his trip report. "He was rather full of himself the rest of the way down."

The ascent of Mount Washington was easier than expected. The "worst weather in the world" was nowhere to be found on a sunny, balmy, and nearly windless Super Bowl Sunday.

Perhaps the most memorable hike of Brutus's second winter round was a 23-mile traverse of Zealand Mountain and the Bond Range in late February. While crossing the open ridge between Mounts Bond and Bondcliff, the group battled 50-mph winds, with gusts into the 70s.

"I steadied Brutus by holding his collar and huddling behind boulders during the worst gusts," recalled Rooney. "Fortunately, everyone made it safely, but we were all bruised a bit from getting knocked down multiple times by the winds. In retrospect, we would never have attempted the hike if we'd known how strong the winds were." Rooney said that Brutus was visibly relieved when that difficult section was over and they were back in the safety of the trees.

"Brutus's emotional reactions to tough situations are much like ours," he said. "You can see the relief he experiences after it's all over: he frisks around a bit immediately afterward."

Over the course of many uphill and downhill miles, Brutus and his owner have developed a strong rapport on the trail that has helped them through dicey spots.

"Brutus and I have hiked so much together that he just gives me a certain type of quick look when he wants some help," said Rooney. "In a tricky area above treeline, I'll tap my hiking pole on rocks to point the way I think will be easiest for him. You can see the wheels churning when I do that. Sometimes he takes that route and sometimes he chooses his own. But it's a lot of fun to know when you're communicating with someone at that level."

This writer had the good fortune to join Kevin, Brutus & Friends on two hikes as they neared the end of their all-forty-eight-in-one-winter quest. A mountain climb with this group is a leisurely outing. When Brutus halts for one of his occasional sprawls in the snow, the entire line of hikers takes a break.

"Brutus is the most energy-efficient hiker I know," said Al Dwyer, a veteran of many treks with Mr. B. "He never wastes any effort."

On a late February trip to Mount Osceola off the Kancamagus Highway, I watched in admiration as Brutus made short work of the steep, grueling pitch up towards the mountain's East Peak. A few days later, my wife Carol and I joined the "Brutus Brigade" for an ascent of Mount Tecumseh in the Waterville Valley. Before hitting the trail, we watched as a WMUR-TV reporter interviewed Rooney for a night time news piece. Brutus struck a majestic pose for the camera, clearly comfortable with his celebrity.

Our group of ten made a slow and jovial climb to the summit, number forty-six on Brutus's all-in-one-winter round. One hiker fed him some hard-boiled eggs, which he washed down with powder snow — his preferred hydration method in winter. Supersize dog biscuits were also on the menu. On the way back, we had a delightful time snowshoeing down the trail behind the bounding, snow-loving Newfie.

We were not able to accompany Brutus up Cannon Mountain on March 6, as he completed his forty-eighth and final summit for the winter of 2004-05. But about forty other hikers did go along, and there was a grand celebration on top, with a banner, a suitably decorated cake, filet mignon for the honoree, and the unveiling of the official "Brutus Brigade" t-shirt.

Never one to rest on his laurels, Brutus was seen out with his owner climbing several more peaks during the last weeks of winter, and many more on into the spring. At a gathering last May, friends and family joined to honor Rooney and Brutus before their planned move to California. The pair received a custom-made miniature rock cairn with Brutus's accomplishments emblazoned upon tiny trail signs. Brutus was also awarded the third-ever "Order of the Golden Biscuit," the ultimate tribute from the Four-Legged Explorers Association (FLEA). The previous two honorees were Barkley Mayer, a frequent contributor to *Appalachia* in the 1990s, (whose human companion, Doug Mayer, is co-author of the Mountain Voices series published regularly in this journal), and Tuckerman Ray (whose human companions are Brad Ray and Rebecca Oreskes, the Mountain Voices co-author.)

Brutus relaxing on North Twin. PHOTO BY KEVIN ROONEY

Though they will be sorely missed by their legions of friends and admirers in New England, Rooney and Brutus will certainly carry on in California. As one friend of Rooney's was heard to predict, it won't be long before there will be a western chapter of the "Brutus Brigade" tramping around the Sierra Nevada.

You just can't keep a good dog down.

Steven D. Smith, whose most recent book is *Wandering Through the White Mountains: A Hiker's Perspective,* is owner of The Mountain Wanderer, a popular bookstore for outdoor types in Lincoln, New Hampshire. He is also coauthor of the *AMC White Mountain Guide* and *Appalachia*'s News and Notes editor.

Aurora Lights Up the Denali Sky

By Bill Sherwonit

O N THE CUSP OF WINTER, I'VE TRAVELED NORTH FROM ANCHORAGE to spend a week in Denali National Park. I spend my days exploring the park's northern foothills and my nights in a log cabin along its eastern edge. Every evening, before retiring, I check the sky. Denali isn't widely known for its beautiful night skies simply because most people visit in summer, when the sky never fully darkens. But local residents know, and I have learned first-hand in recent years, that for eight or nine months of every twelve, many of the park's most inspiring spectacles are to be found overhead.

What grabs a sky-gazer's attention on most of these clear, dark nights are the sparkling stars, the familiar constellations, the Milky Way band. On moonless nights, the ink-black sky grows vibrantly alive with uncountable numbers of sparkling stars. With no urban glare to dim their intensity, they blink brightly, wildly, like Christmas tree lights or fireflies. Occasionally, however, Denali's night sky holds other luminous mysteries.

One evening toward the end of my stay, it is moonless and clear, filled with sparkling stars and the faintest trace of northern lights. I watch a while, hoping for an auroral burst, but the lights fade and I head to bed.

Hours later I awaken from a restless sleep. Remembering the earlier display I stumble, blurry-eyed, to a large picture window that faces west. Just above the darkened Alaska Range foothills, a pale, green band arches gently across the sky, like a flattened rainbow. The arc seems to be flickering but at first I'm not sure if it's the aurora borealis or my eyes. I rub them and watch more intently. Now there's no question: the band is slowly wavering. This goes on for five or ten minutes. Then the aurora explodes and fills the whole western sky. Bright green curtains of northern lights, tinged pink along their edges, ripple wildly above the hills. I've seen northern lights many times, but I am shocked by the deep, flashing brilliance of these.

The bright curtains abruptly vanish, leaving as suddenly and mysteriously as they first appeared, but faint patches and bands remain. Paler than the original green arc, they nearly disappear, then grow more intense. Now they are shimmering and jumping around the sky. My mind tries to put words to what I'm seeing, to make them more comprehensible.

The lights shimmer, flicker, pulsate. They ripple, explode, undulate. At times they are the embers of a heavenly fire, flickering on and off. At other times they are flames, leaping across the sky. There are moments when they remind me of exploding fireworks. An electric arc. Cannon fire. Or psyche-

Northern Lights, Denali National Park, Alaska. PHOTO BY JOHNNY JOHNSON/ALASKASTOCK.COM.

delic lights, of the kind used in discos. Now they are rippling waves that appear at the horizon and move across an oceanic sky. They are the shimmer of sunlight on a river or a lightly rippled lake.

These northern lights hypnotize me in a way that few others have. I lose track of time. How long have I watched? An hour? Two? I recently finished John Muir's *Travels in Alaska*, which includes a chapter on the aurora. Never one to avoid discomfort—or an adventure—Muir in 1890 witnessed an unusually dramatic aurora borealis display in southeast Alaska: "Losing all thought of sleep, I ran back to my cabin, carried out blankets, and lay down on the (glacial) moraine to keep watch until daybreak, that none of the sky wonders of the glorious night within reach of my eyes might be lost."

I too think about going outside. But the view is good from here and I don't wish to pile on clothes or watch the sky in 20-degree cold. I'm content to sit inside, with bare feet, short-sleeve shirt, and sweatpants. I lean against the window for several minutes at a time; when shoulder and upper back muscles stiffen, I move to a nearby armchair.

I tell myself to simply sit and watch and appreciate the aurora. No description, no analysis. It's hard to do. Words and images keep coming to mind. I think about the origins of northern lights and the science that explains them. Researchers tell us that these auroral apparitions are atmospheric phenomena, produced when a stream of charged particles from the sun, known as the solar wind, intersects the Earth's magnetic field. While most of the solar particles are deflected, some filter down into the planet's upper atmosphere, where they collide with gas molecules such as nitrogen and oxygen. The resulting reactions produce glowing colors. The aurora most commonly is pale green, but at times its borders are tinged with pink, purple, or red. Especially rare is the all-red aurora, which appears when charged solar particles collide with high-altitude oxygen. The science is complex and difficult to comprehend, but the results are pure beauty.

I appreciate the insights that scientists have gained in recent years and their improved ability to predict auroral events. Our Anchorage newspaper presents nightly auroral forecasts and directs readers to an aurora website. But on a night like this, with wild fiery lights burning across the Denali sky, I eventually—perhaps inevitably—choose rhapsody over rational thought, poetry over physical phenomena. These lights hint of forces larger than we can imagine, of worlds beyond our physical one.

In my watching, I begin to see a rhythm in the flashing, flickering, shimmering lights. Or at least I imagine one. I can also imagine why the peoples of so many northern cultures have created myths to explain the aurora. The lights take on a life, an energy, of their own. What began as patches, arcs, bands, curtains, and spirals has been transformed. Now the lights are wispy, vaporous, human-like figures in the sky, drumming and dancing and singing. At other times, lights exploding along the horizon are the traces of distant battles.

The lights are still flashing and pulsating when I return to bed. While I don't have Muir's all-night stamina, like him more than a century ago I've been touched in unforgettable ways by the "sky wonders" of a glorious northern night. Shining beacons, they urge me to pay attention to the wildness and mystery that surrounds me—both here in Denali and back home in Anchorage—and also lives inside me.

BILL SHERWONIT, a nature writer and resident of Anchorage since 1982, is the author of ten books about Alaska. His website is www.billsherwonit.alaskawriters.com.

On the Glacier

Cold spun the hours
thin as cotton candy

and dark carved
impatience into bites.

We were bred
out of the glacier, two stick

figures in a slick of soft
ice, a crevice by the ton

cinching our legs and a sky
ready to crack.

Just when we needed
a handhold,

the wavering light
slipped through our fingers.

We skinned ourselves, pickaxe
and rope, across the surface.

The air had lungs and ribs. It
congealed our blood

in droplets, waited
at the glacier's edge with our breath.

The mountain shrugged us off
without looking,

let us carry the frostbite home
for a bouquet,

purple leaves, white buds sprouting
at our fingertips.

—*James Doyle*

JAMES DOYLE's latest book is *Einstein Considers a Sand Dune* (Steel Toe Books, 2004), the winner of the 2003 Steel Toe Book Contest. He has published poems in many journals, including *Alaska Quarterly Review*, *Cold Mountain Review*, *The Iowa Review*, and *Poetry*. His piece "Severe Aunts" was read on National Public Radio by Garrison Keillor in 2004.

The 4,000-Footers in Winter

"They're Beautiful, They're out There, and They're Calling Me"

By Timothy Muskat

Non sum qualis eram (I am not what once I was).
—Horace, *Odes*

i

In December 2003, I set alone to climb New Hampshire's forty-eight 4,000-footers. That's the story of my winter—or at least the trajectory of it. There are the facts, of course, and the numbers: 22 hikes, 48 mountains, 283.1 total miles. Sometimes in crampons; sometimes in snowshoes; sometimes as a post-holing fool. At times, I encountered dangerous conditions; always, there was the bone-tingling cold. On twenty of my twenty-two hikes, I saw not a soul. On forty-three of the summits I reached, I stood half-stalwart, half-shivering, half-achingly alone. As my wife put it, I was untethered and uncompanioned. I didn't set out to accomplish anything; I simply freed myself for the mountains.

ii

To go up into the desolate isolation of mountains into what one can only call the mountains' truest interior is to know the nature of isolation itself—that ineffable, unmappable place where the tree will sometimes fall, and space and time recede. Where knowledge, and the urge for knowledge, falls away. When you add in winter, you are forced to consider what it truly means to be alone. Alone in the mountains in winter, you become something apart, something sheathed. The Latin, *insula*, from which our "isolation" derives, nicely describes a blanketing of snow across a landscape.

iii

What was lost: weight; feeling in toes and several critical fingers (damage unretractable); any sense of imperiousness or brashness, or of needing to be somewhere fast; and any notion that I could be more than a momentary presence in a landscape unhumanly grand.

What was gained is harder to measure. Perspective: everything in the winter mountains enlarges, intensifies. You learn to see and appreciate all you might have missed in balmier times—shapes, contours, peculiar outcroppings of detritus and rock. Even abstractions become clearer: *elevation gain* and the nuances of *up*. The ramifications—you feel it in your legs—of *traverse*. I learned to fall. I gained the talent of wanting nothing in particular, save an occasional swallow of water or the gift of a morning without wind.

Monroe, near dusk, in the company of no-nonsense cairns. PHOTO BY TIMOTHY MUSKAT

iv

I'd arrive at a trailhead at 4:00 A.M.—nothing around but cold and my own-most dread of it. Like a man being parent to himself, I would force myself to get a *move on*. There was always a reluctance to get going: I had almost to throw myself into it. But I was never quite sure I had the strength or the temerity to go forward. In winter mountains, your sense of going is summarily diminished to the commonplace *one small step at a time*. But small steps become motion, and motion pulls. I was a man determined to push onward without ever knowing where *onward* might lead.

v

If I could give reasons—if I could say I did it *because*—I'm fairly sure no one would be in the slightest way interested or edified. I have always appreciated wild places, and since I was about knee-high have favored solitude over company, thought over action, nature over—no offense—humankind.

But why again and again? Thoreau says curiosity is the highest form of knowledge, and that's good enough for me. At root I was curious: I wanted to see what things looked like in winter. And I wanted to see if I *could* do it,

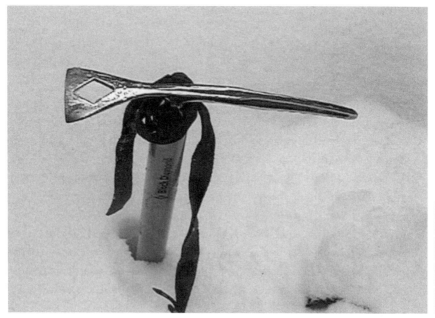

Job security: an ice axe on Owl's Head summit atop a snowy cairn.

if I had in me something of the Spenserian knight errant—a character who takes on travail while another (a warm, hearthside reader, say) observes from safer vantage. Whatever adventure or mishap befell me would be altogether my own. I could leave footprints—runelike—for some other winter walker to find, ponder, and decode. I was going out and up into winter because it seemed the only way to discover what was actually there.

vi

The climbing of mountains never ends, because climbing is continuous: you go up and over, and up and over again. This repetition, driven by the *need* to climb again, is hard to explain. No true mountaineer heads upward in a spirit of conquest—a heavily laden term burdened by implications of *against*. Rather, the climbing itself is the main event, and the randomness of climbing is part of its attractiveness.

When I reached my forty-eighth and final winter summit in the Whites, the magnetic Mount Hale, I felt a certain elation of attainment. But I was also overcome by a nagging sense that completion was the least fulfilling thing of all. Two hours later, exhausted and thawing in my slow-warming car, I wanted only to get back up there.

vii

Nowhere do the tragic and the laughable come together more poignantly than in a spruce trap. I fell into several. The most tenacious was on the Carter–Moriah Trail, just past its junction with the Black Angel. The tearing-loose took several minutes, in which I found myself shouting, like a Keatsian priestess, in several different tongues.

The most terrifying was in a dense conifer thicket roughly halfway between the summits of Mounts Davis and Isolation. I had been bushwhacking (it was February, and the Isolation Trail from the Rocky Branch junction onward was impassable) when suddenly I felt myself plummet. One moment I was up and walking, the next I was down—deep down—and utterly confined. Imagine yourself trapped in a man-sized medicine capsule the top of which has been lopped off. Then imagine having to free yourself without the use of your arms. That'll give you some idea of my predicament. As I struggled to extricate myself—spruce traps seem to be, in a horror film-like way, alive—I lost my left snowshoe completely. So when I eventually got myself out after about

An unusual shamrock shape on Mt Madison.

half an hour of tunneling and exertion, in a temperature my tiny thermometer told me was roughly 14 degrees, I had to go back *in*—head-first—to retrieve that orphaned shoe.

viii

When the dew point—the temperature at which a vapor begins to condense—and the temperature drop to the same level, you get 100-percent humidity, which can spell disaster for the winter climber. It did for Ken Holmes, the part-time ranger who died two winters back on the Twinway. It got so humid, so wet, so *January*, that Holmes's clothing no longer served to wick the moisture from his body. And when the temperature shot downward, the vexing daylong wet combined with the unforeseen evening cold killed him.

I happened to be on the Twinway about ten days before Holmes perished there, and I ran into the same scientific phenomenon. Only in my case, the temperature was more cooperative: it hovered throughout my twelve-hour day at around 29 degrees. But by the time I'd slogged my way up and over North Twin, South Twin, and Galehead and plodded my way back toward the North Twin access road along the North Twin trail, my boots, my beautiful, protective, two-paycheck, Italian-made, winter climbing boots, were filled with water. Several miles and a difficult stream-crossing from my car, walking in the pitch dark through a nearly inaudible winter rain, I could barely see and, worse, barely acknowledge, the landscape before me.

I came round a bend in the trail, and there he was, smack in the middle of everything. I was overcome on the spot—by terror, wonder, awe. So I barked, as I imagined a beagle might, at a neighbor's cat. It was the petty, domestic sound that came to me out there. And my first moose, startled, ran.

ix

I went up the Crawford Path into just-emerging daylight thinking *Abel Ethan Abel*, sky tingling the treetops and tinting the whitened landscape a strange and shimmering iridescence that was mine alone to know and savor. Perhaps Abel and Ethan—bless them for cutting this historic trail—knew it once, too. When I came to treeline, I could see the wondrously globular shape of Eisenhower, picture-like in the near-distance, with Washington, a giant quavering bell, pealing in the backdrop. I'd almost forgotten it was 24 below. But no way was I turning back. Whatever wind and ice had in store for me farther on, whatever you might ascribe to me in the way of stupidity or foolishness, I was going forward.

x

I staggered along the Webster Cliff Trail to Mount Jackson, a bitterly cold day's final prize. I was chilled to the marrow. My toes and thin-gloved fingers had gone numb, and I could feel by reaching up to touch them that my frost-bitten cheeks had bubbled and scabbed. Stabbing my poles harpoon-like in the deep banks of snow to either side of me, I swung my pack off my back and found enough presence of mind to wrench from the topmost pouch a plastic bag half-filled with almonds and assorted nuts.

As I fumbled to feed myself, something flickered into view. It was a gray jay, common in these parts, even in winter, and it had alighted on the burled handle of one of my upright poles. It looked at me clownishly, cocking its ruffled head. Then it leapt—jumped, really—into the exposed upper vault of my pack. Half dazed, this acrobatic visitant only inches away, I shook a single peanut from the bag and held it aloft in one near-frozen hand. On the instant, the bird fluttered up out of the pack, swooped down into my hand,

and gobbled up the offered nut. This easy give-and-take went on for some time. He ate and I ate. Never in my life had I felt so rewarded, so comforted by the *presence* of something. That bird was solicitude. He dissuaded me from my own worst self. I resolved to get on with it, to push myself through snow and cold to Mount Jackson and beyond.

xi

In the mountains in wintertime, you learn to accept—you're forced to accept—discomfort. The outside limit of discomfort is misery—the coming together of cold and wind and snow and fear and uncertainty and tiredness—it happens all at once, and you just can't fathom what to do. The mountains in winter changed me and my sea-level notion of things irrevocably and forever.

You also never know precisely where you are in time. The space you're in—tingly, stark, indomitable—predominates. Its vastness absorbs you. And fatigue plays tricks with your mind. I stumbled down the Gorge Brook Trail just off the wind-blasted summit of Moosilauke as a crepuscular darkness came on, and I came upon someone's insulated canteen lying top-down in the snow. Who had dropped it? I wondered. And why hadn't I noticed it on my way up, only an hour before? Was there a waterless soul lost and wandering somewhere off trail? Should I try to save him? Only when I reached to pick it up did I realize this bright red vessel was mine and that it must have fallen from my waist as I was laboring up old Moosilauke through knee-deep snow.

xii

Conrad Gesner was a sixteenth-century naturalist who was determined, solely for the sake of his "mental delight," to climb at least one peak every year. And though his determination quickly waned, and he never actually followed through with his plan, Gesner became the first of the zanies, characters who simply want to get to a mountain's top presumably, like the bear in the well-known parable, to see what one can see.

I am half a Gesner, I guess. I had the determination to summit but could see no delight in it. I knew from the outset that if I was going to knock forty-eight of them off in a single winter I would have to do it entirely on guts and fear.

It's late January. I am making my way up North Tripyramid's treacherous slide, and I find myself about midway stapled to a slab of ice roughly the size of a sofa cushion. I'm on a section of trail the guidebooks tell me should be considered hazardous in winter and should, therefore, be avoided. Nonetheless, on this cushion-sized slab of ice I am adjusting a wayward crampon while trying to find one small, natural nubbin on which to loop my walking poles so that I can swing my pack from my back to my front, brace it against my left thigh, and find the high-energy bar I remember—or think I remember—putting in the night before. The wind is roaring. A light snow, circumambient, contributes to the confusion. It's a recipe for disaster. Bracing myself and unable, alas, to do anything with my walking poles but tuck them under one arm, I swing my pack around. With the motion, my poles go cartwheeling down the slide. Twenty yards down, one of them catches on a tiny gnarl of—what is that, a sprig of sapling beech? Twenty yards farther, the other pole catches, balancing like gymnast or butterfly on a smidgen of exposed rock. The poles, which I have now to retrieve, do not lie in accessible paths. *Addendum for trail guide, note to self:* If innately foolish, and intent on climbing, against all good advice, North Tripyramid Slide in winter, wait for a reasonably flat spot before adjusting crampon and deciding you're hungry.

No wonder Conrad Gesner elected to stay indoors.

Two trees conferring in full view of Tripyramid's North Slide.

PHOTO BY TIMOTHY MUSKAT

xiii

When you meet someone in the mountains, it is inexpressibly *not* like an everyday encounter: it's not the mail carrier coming down the street, or the stranger acknowledging you with a friendly wave, or your neighbor, missed for a week or two, reentering the picture with "Hey, buddy, have you seen today's front page?" No, it is like coming upon yourself: coming around a bend where pine boughs are thick with weeks of snow to see precisely what you yourself must look like. It's your hibernal *other*.

xiv

When I was a boy I was delivered into the White Mountains by my father, who believed that an early immersion in mountain climbing would build in his oldest son character, self-reliance, a Dutch kind of courage, and an appreciation for what might be called the usefulness — my father was a Quaker — of diligence, resiliency, and focused work. You worked up a mountain and you worked your way back down. Then you celebrated the work.

What I found in my winter climbing, however, some forty years after my first working trek up Chocorua, was that the mountains don't care a farthing

One of the White Mountains' more whimsical signs.

for effort, focus, diligence, self-reliance or—the work of it notwithstanding—who or what you think you are. My father's ennobled vision was a purely human construct. What the mountains finally made me understand is precisely what I've been teaching students of poetry for years: mountains, like poems, lead us to unknown, irrational, unyoked parts of our being, and then, like poems, lead us *back* to the known, rational, connected parts of ourselves—but refreshed, revivified, and sometimes changed.

xv

In everything beautiful, says Hopkins, there is something regular and irregular; something symmetrical and asymmetrical; something alike and something dissimilar. At the heart of beauty, in other words, is contrast, relation, balance. The oak is beautiful because its branches are gnarled, unruly and ruggedly irregular while its crown (formed by those very same branches) makes across the skyline a smooth, overarching, almost mathematically drawn inverted bowl. Painters see it. *Beautiful,* we say in passing, sensing but not entirely conscious of the contrast that makes it so.

xvi

The secret I took away from the winter mountains: endure and be willing. We can learn from the dignity and self-restraint of mountains. They don't presuppose. I can't say conclusively, like Dogen, that mountains talk among themselves while we sleep. But I live for that possibility, and I'm going to keep my winter-nipped ears open from here on out.

TIMOTHY MUSKAT, 44, is a poet and former English professor who lives in Sandwich, New Hampshire, with his wife and their two sons. In 2003–4, after recovering from serious back surgery, he climbed all forty-eight of New Hampshire's 4,000-footers in a single winter—and last winter went out and did it again. He plans to try his luck a third time this winter, because "they're beautiful, they're out there, and they're calling me."

Two Camps in Three Acts

Yesterday and Today at Crag Camp and Gray Knob

By Robert Kruszyna

Prologue

It certainly was a special occasion to be invited, in late November 1953, for a weekend at Crag Camp* by the "Johns." At that time, John Perry, John Shugrue, and John Post (along with John Taylor, who was then in the service) were the preeminent leaders in the AMC rock-climbing program, which I had just joined. Unlike today's specialists, who scorn walking more than 100 yards to the cliffs, or practice their sport indoors in a climbing gym, the rock climbers of the 1950s were all-around outdoorsmen, participating in hiking, camping, canoeing, skiing, and above all, winter climbing and snowshoeing, as necessary preludes to mountaineering in the greater ranges. To be included in such august company after just a few skirmishes on the Greater Boston crags was nearly overwhelming to an eager would-be mountaineer of 22.

On Saturday evening at Crag Camp, with John Post (who studied composition under Walter Piston at Harvard) improvising sinister sounds on the pipe organ, we read *Macbeth*, each taking on a role. As the fire dwindled, old and not-so-old tales were related, in particular one about an unexpected descent of King Ravine's Great Gully. On a winter ascent a year earlier, Perry and Shugrue were returning at dusk across the top of King Ravine, when Shugrue lost his footing in the wind and started to slide down the Great Gully. In his efforts to self-arrest, his ice axe was torn from his hands and he slid headfirst down the length of the Gully. In the dim light, Perry carefully descended the snow, picking up Shugrue's axe on the way. He found his friend at the bottom, unharmed but thoroughly shaken—an experience from which Shugrue's confidence never recovered. Little did I guess that the outcome of my next trip to Crag Camp would turn on this episode.

Act I

Only three months later, several of the "tigers" in the Tufts Mountain Club decided to organize a major trip to the White Mountains during the February break. Our objective was to traverse Mounts Adams, Jefferson, and Clay and arrive at the peak of Mount Washington—then to return. In the winter of 1954, no one had yet traversed the Northern Presidentials in winter, let alone make it all the way to Mount Washington. Such is the naïve self-confidence of the young.

---

*Crag Camp and its companion, Gray Knob, are cabins on the north side of Mount Adams just below treeline at an elevation of about 4,200 feet.

Opposite: Winter at the old Crag Camp in 1978. PHOTO BY HARRIET KRUSZYNA

Since I had led a successful trip based at the old Harvard Cabin* in December, Tufts Mountain Club officials asked me to lead this one. They were interested in tempering the undirected enthusiasm of some of the younger hikers. After all, I was experienced, having been to Crag Camp, and I was *mature*, being at that time a graduate student.

In those days, before interstates and turnpikes, it was a very long drive from Boston up Route 16 to Randolph, New Hampshire. After starting the evening before, it was mid-morning when our hearse pulled in to Boothman's driveway. (Before the advent of minivans and SUVs, a second-hand hearse proved ideal transportation for climbing groups.) The sage of Randolph, Jack Boothman came out to inquire about our plans, and as was his wont, offered information and advice about trail conditions, weather, and so forth. It seemed we could expect maybe one more good day. After a lot of tooling up, the eight of us, heavily laden, started up the Amphibrach.

For the most part, we wore World War II–surplus clothing. Army ski pants, durable and wind-resistant, were a prized favorite, along with oversized GI boots with lots of socks, and a tent-weight cotton anorak, colored white for camouflage. Not easy to see one's companions in a white-out! Our packs were steel-framed Army rucksacks, those fiendishly impractical sacks in which all the contents formed a heavy lump located 6 inches behind one's rump. The Tenth Mountain Division snowshoes were the one truly serviceable piece of equipment. Indeed, I still use a pair on occasion.

Needless to say, the trail was not broken out, but with several of us breaking, we made decent progress. Our way lay up the New Spur Trail, the now-abandoned lower part of the Old Spur Trail, to which the present route has been re-relocated. It was nearly dark when we reached Crag Camp, started a fire, set up dinner, and reorganized for the morrow's big push. In those days, firewood was laid in for the winter months. It was a near-luxurious advance base camp high in the mountains.

Act II

Even so, it was a cold job crawling out of one's Army surplus sleeping bag in the morning and getting ready for the day's adventure. After much discussion, we decided to forgo snowshoes, which would be a nuisance as soon

---

*This cabin, long since demolished, was located just off the Sherburne Ski Trail not far from the Tuckerman Ravine complex.

as we reached treeline. Everyone had crampons, mostly the "wrought iron" Army variety, and either a wooden ice axe or ski poles. Maybe because I was an incipient mountaineer, I had thrown a manila rope into my already over-loaded pack. It lent the appropriate sense of seriousness to the venture.

To post-hole the several hundred feet up through the remaining trees was something of a struggle, but once we reached the wind-blown, rock-strewn slopes above, we were glad we didn't have to carry snowshoes, which act as a sail in the wind.

Surprisingly, everything progressed according to plan. The pace *did* become ever slower after we began the long pull from Edmands Col to the summit of Mount Jefferson. The party, likely too large to start with, was also too disparate in terms of energy and stamina.

Nevertheless, we continued on uneventfully, if painfully slowly, to the summit of Mount Clay. It was already mid-afternoon; in February that means no more than two hours of daylight remaining. There before us rose Mount Washington—high above us and a long, long way off. The sky to the south-west was turning an ominous black. Two of the party had clearly reached their physical limits. Also, it would a long grind going back over or around Jefferson. Despite the eagerness I could see in the eyes of the two fittest members, and my own ambition, I said, "It's time to go back."

PHOTO ROBERT KRUSZYNA

Looking north from Mt. Adams.

As we headed up from Edmands Col to the place on Mount Adams now asininely called "Thunderstorm Junction," it began to snow—a heavy, wet, blinding snow. By the time we crawled into the lee of what may have been Mount Adams, it was dark. I say "may have been" because I knew we were lost—lost, wet, cold, tired, and *frightened*. Now I understood why had I had lugged that heavy rope all day. With the help of Howie and Bill, I tied the party in, not so much for protection but so we would not get separated. I put Howie at one end, Bill in the middle, and myself in the lead at the other end. Indeed, without the stout assistance of those two, we would probably all have died. It is a bitter commentary on our present times that we never considered splitting the party, whereas nowadays the stronger save themselves by leaving the weaker to die.

Somewhere out there in front of us, in the darkness and swirling snow, I knew the Great Gully fell away into the depths of the ravine. Keep bearing left, *left*, my inner voice cried. So we did, eventually reaching the first trees and a semblance of safety. Reconstructing our course, I think we missed our upward path and entered the krummholz in the shallow depression between Nowell Ridge and the sharp ridge on which Crag Camp stands. We were more or less safe, but definitely not out of it yet. I plunged into the dense forest, tunneling through snow up to my chin, dragging my companions after me. In those years, it really snowed in these mountains! This arduous exercise seemed to last forever, but after losing perhaps 1,000 feet of elevation, we arrived in more open forest. I am now reasonably certain we crossed the Gray Knob Trail in passing, but, since it was not snowshoed out (as it always is nowadays), we didn't see it. It must be remembered that many of these surmises are *post facto*; at the time, I was ignorant, inexperienced, and otherwise unfamiliar with the terrain.

When we found a stream, presumably Spur Brook, we decided in good woodsman's fashion to follow it down. The rope had now become a handicap, so we took it off. We reversed order, with Howie in the vanguard and myself at the rear. At one point, I stumbled into what I thought was a snow-covered tree, only to discover it was one of my companions. He was truly invisible in his white anorak. He had sat down to rest and dozed off, the prelude to hypothermic death. Thoroughly roused by the point of my ice axe, he tottered on.

It was about 4:00 A.M. when we finally staggered into Boothman's dooryard. In spite of the hour, Jack and Gwen greeted us with immense concern and solicitude. They took us in, bedded us down on the floor, provided us with blankets, and Gwen served us hot soup. None of us has forgotten that

PHOTO BY ROBERT KRUSZYNA

Great Gully in King Ravine. The site where John Shugrue lost his footing and his ice axe in 1953. He slid headfirst down the length of the Gully. Fortunately, he was unharmed.

kindness and support. Late the following morning, four of us went back up the hill to recover the sleeping bags, snowshoes, and other gear left behind at Crag Camp. Such is the unbounded energy of the young.

Interlude

In the succeeding years, I returned numerous times to Crag Camp and later to Gray Knob as the focus shifted there. In all those trips, only once did we share the cabin with another party. Quite a difference from today's palatial facilities and their overcrowding! My last trip to Crag was with my wife Harriet in the late 1960s. By this time, the cabin was an empty shell, no more firewood, no stoves, no pipe organ. It was merely basic shelter, and barely that, as the wind kept blowing the door open during the night. On that occasion, we did complete the traverse over Mount Washington and down to Pinkham Notch. A few years later, we moved permanently to Randolph, making the mountainside cabins superfluous. As a matter of fact, there is not a major peak in the White Mountains, save possibly Mount Bond, that cannot be climbed and descended in winter in one day from the road.

Act III

For Christmas 2003, Harriet and I gave each other a night at Gray Knob: accommodation, two lunches, breakfast, and dinner with a glass of wine. All for 10 dollars per person. Both of the original cabins, Gray Knob and Crag Camp, dating from the early years of the twentieth century, were razed in recent years and replaced with new, modern versions, which nonetheless retain some of the layout and character of the older camps, including a new pipe organ in Crag Camp (now, however, it is securely locked up except for the use of notables of the Randolph Mountain Club, which operates the huts).

Nostalgia motivated our trip: it was the 50th anniversary of my first, 1953, trip to Crag Camp. At that time, *anyone* could play the old pipe organ. Then too, both camps were heated in winter, Crag in particular sporting an oil-drum barrel woodstove that glowed in the dark and a four-clawed, cast-iron wood cook stove. It presented a fire hazard, no doubt, but it was comfortable, too. In that era, the woodstove in Gray Knob mostly smoked.

For this 2003 winter visit, I had planned a trip that would involve going up to Gray Knob, spending the night, climbing Mount Adams the following day, then descending to the Randolph Valley. We were able to enlist the support of Nick Grossoehme, a graduate Dartmouth graduate student with some hiking experience, who was enthusiastic about doing his first winter climb.

On Sunday morning, December 14, at 0 degrees Fahrenheit, we started up Lowe's Path. Nick was carrying 45 pounds, Harriet 25, and I 35. Although we carried both snowshoes and crampons, the path had been broken out, so we didn't need either, despite a snow depth of some 20 inches. It took us more than four hours to hump the 3,000 feet to Gray Knob. The weather had been gradually deteriorating, as forecast, but we had some good views, which excited Nick. Gray Knob was empty; the caretaker was on a "valley run." The temperature inside the cabin was 20 degrees Fahrenheit, we were damp from sweat, and the woodstove was padlocked! The RMC truly meters out the BTUs.

To stay warm, we made a short excursion upwards to treeline so Nick could take some "I was there" photos. Then we post-holed over to Crag Camp to experience the sensational view into King Ravine. Wisely, along the way, we filled our 5-gallon plastic water jug from the spring that is one-half mile round-trip from the hut.

In the meantime, the forerunner of another party had arrived, and Tom had holed up in his sleeping bag. Fatalistically, we tooled up for our dinner. Butane stoves do not burn very hot in such cold temperatures, and because Nick, like all the younger generation who live on bottled, "pure" water, was concerned about water safety, it took a long time to boil any. Then the directions on the packaged soup said, "Add boiling water, stir thoroughly, close the flap, and let sit for ten minutes". . . by that time, it would have frozen. Likewise the directions for the freeze-dried lasagna, our main course. So we ate a lot of partially reconstituted roughage, which was not great, since we were already somewhat dehydrated. But the cheap California burgundy I had lugged up took an edge off our misery.

The rest of the other group arrived, a disparate bunch of 40-pluses on a "guys' night out." Dedicated winter climbers and maintaining old relationships with each other, they were having a great time. Eventually, Adam, the caretaker arrived and quickly started a fire. By the time we went to bed at the early hour of 9:00 P.M., the inside temperature had reached a sultry 40 degrees Fahrenheit. But the early lack of heat had eliminated much of the camaraderie and conversation that I remembered as an enjoyable part of such trips in the old days.

Meanwhile, the anticipated storm had arrived in its full fury. The wind howled, the snow swirled around the hut. To go outside to take a leak became nearly a life-or-death proposition. But I was so dehydrated that it proved unnecessary. It's amazing how warm those down sleeping bags are. Once Harriet applied some commercial foot-warmers to my feet, I was never cold.

According to RMC strictures, there is no heat in the morning, so breakfast followed the same shivering scenario as dinner the night before. We had hoped that we might have an opportunity to climb Mount Adams, 1,600-feet above us. But the high wind, the snow coming in horizontally, the lack of visibility, and the wind-packed and ice-glazed snow underfoot persuaded us to go down. Down sounds easy, but 25 inches of new snow adds significant new effort. Nick, and sometimes Tom, beat out the trail, but Harriet and I nevertheless consumed a lot of energy in flailing in the deep, new snow.

When it was over, Nick, tired though he was, waxed enthusiastic about his first winter climbing experience. I was physically exhausted but nonetheless satisfied with what may well have been my last.

Epilogue

Now, after 50-plus seasons of mountaineering and hundreds of alpine climbs, several of them involving more desperate situations than here recorded, I recognize how important that long-ago episode at Crag Camp was to my subsequent climbing career. One lesson particularly stands out: when you undertake risky activities, you're on your own. It is imperative to bring to the venture the physical and psychological resources to cope with whatever unexpected and potentially disastrous circumstances arise. Too bad that fundamental requirement is so widely ignored.

Bob and Harriet Kruszyna have just completed their 51st and 44th seasons of mountaineering by climbing a few peaks in the Alps. Their final outdoor objective is to *not* climb Owl's Head, their one remaining 4,000-footer.

Snow Geese

Down from the north they fly,
sharp arrows in the hue of winter.

At the intersection of paths
along the river, flocks sink

in wave after wave, sowing
the fields with feathers and sound.

A heavy burden they tow, memory
of cold and ice, to a mild, fertile heartland.

What would it take to set those wings
again in the sky, to see the screens of white

rise before our eyes, snow lift itself back
off the ground to rejoin the clouds?

—Susan Edwards Richmond

SUSAN EDWARDS RICHMOND's poems have appeared in *Blueline*, *Green Mountains Review*, *Wild Earth*, and *Sanctuary: The Journal of the Massachusetts Audubon Society*. Her chapbook, *Boto*, was published by Adastra Press in 2002.

Laying Waste to the Land to Produce Electricity

Rupert River Project Could Be an Important Tipping Point

By Paul Rudershausen

I MAGINE THAT THE DESTRUCTION OF A NATIVE AMERICAN CULTURE and its vast wilderness was occurring today and not in a chapter of North American history. Imagine that this eradication of virgin forests and miles of wild rivers was happening just a day's drive from New York and New England. And because this devastation was wrought by a Quebec government corporation selling electricity into your home, imagine that you could help save these native North Americans. Well, imagine no more, for the saga of the Cree Indians is unfolding today in eastern Canada. Northeastern U.S. power suppliers have contracted to buy power from provincially owned Hydro Quebec (HQ), an electric development firm that desires to impound every free-flowing river of central Quebec and, by so doing, eliminate the wild rivers and lakes absolutely essential to the Cree way of life.

For millennia, Cree Indians lived entirely off fish and game they collected from the boreal region of central Canada. Beginning in the 1600s, the centuries-old trade with the Hudson Bay Company solidified their connection with—and dependence on—the massive rivers flowing to Hudson and James bays. The LaGrande, Eastmain, Rupert, and other wild rivers provided fish, game, and routes of travel to important bay trading sites. Until 30 years ago, most of the Cree throughout their 140,000 square-mile territory were subsisting largely off the resources provided by these free-flowing waters. Lakes and rivers dictated the annual cycle of fishing during summer and trapping during winter. All this abruptly changed starting in the 1970s, when HQ commenced its history of destructive hydro projects and broken promises of controlling development and providing compensation to the Cree for damage to their homeland.

The Rupert, considered the southernmost true wilderness river in North America, is gravely threatened by a project to dam and divert up to 90 percent

Hydroelectric damming projects threaten to alter wilderness rivers and forests. Hydro Quebec (HQ) is an electric development firm that desires to impound every free-flowing river of central Quebec.

of its flow. The 2001 deal between the province and Cree politicians has left the river's existence and the future of the Cree hanging in the balance. People from the Cree villages remain deeply divided over whether the agreement will allow them to continue their way of life and protect the rest of the land. Only time will tell, but these Cree have had to make a choice among limited options because of HQ's desire to develop the region.

On two-month canoe trips down the Rupert with a Cree man from Mistassini Village, I have seen for myself what is at stake. This Cree explained to me how the lower half of the west-flowing river, where we netted sturgeon, would at certain times turn into a waterless ditch once HQ began to divert the Rupert's flow to a generating station hundreds of miles to the north. He told me how artificially fluctuating water levels upstream and downstream of a Rupert dam would destroy populations of fur-bearing animals on which the Cree depend. And by showing me maps of the Cree territory and HQ diversion schemes, he demonstrated how damming the Rupert will forever alter central Quebec as new roads and reservoirs pierce their way into a retreating wilderness.

HQ's current plans leave more at stake than just the Rupert. Currently hanging in the balance: the free flow of four massive wilderness waterways

Local grafitti speaks to public concerns regarding watershed damage.

and more than 160 lakes; the survival of Rupert River speckled trout and sturgeon populations; and virgin forests of black spruce now threatened by road building, clear-cutting, and drowning at the bottom of reservoirs. Not surprisingly, experts believe that the removal of up to 85 percent of the Rupert's flow will eliminate most of the natural functions of the watershed, both upstream of the diversion and also downstream in the James Bay estuary. Irrevocable damage will occur as soon as the Rupert is reduced to an almost dry gulch. Internet photos display HQ's history of dewatering the larger Eastmain River to meet foreign electric demands. (See www.ottertooth.com/ Native_K/eastmain_death2.htm)

HQ's past projects in Quebec, like damming and diverting the Eastmain, LaGrande, Caniapiscau, and Sakami rivers, have failed to sustain permanent jobs or economic growth in the Cree land. Damming of the LaGrande River, for example, has poisoned fishes and the Cree with high levels of mercury. And dams have decimated populations of fish and fur-bearing animals. In *Strangers Devour the Land* (Douglas & McIntyre, 1991), Boyce Richardson details the ecological and cultural destruction wrought by corporations that never considered how massive water diversions would devastate a people that has lived off the land for thousands of years.

Across the continent, Indians have been forced from their native lands to reservations, with a predictable loss of culture and autonomy. When considering the impending destruction to the Rupert watershed, it is possible to imagine the unlikely but hoped-for possibility that resource-hungry government interests will finally recognize the importance of a healthy land to the sovereignty of native Americans. The nature of Hydro Quebec's careless treatment of the Cree and a ballooning American demand for cheap electricity leads me to believe that the battle to save the Rupert represents a tipping point not only for the Cree but for the essence of HQ operations to follow. Little about the behavior of provincial Quebec over the last three decades indicates its concern for the importance of wild, unpolluted lakes and rivers to the Cree culture. To the contrary, the past 30 years have exposed the province's practice of eluding legally binding responsibilities to the Cree in the wake of their forced agreement. The outcome of HQ projects has included degraded fishing and hunting opportunities critical to the Cree as well as unkept promises of compensation and responsible development. In a protracted, force-fed adjustment to the twenty-first century, the Cree have faced a destructive corporate takeover of some of their most sacred land.

Along our 400-mile paddling journey last summer I ran into an HQ employee that informed me of the company's new plans to dam the magnificent Great Whale River further north, which a group of New York consumers helped to save from impoundment less than a decade ago. It struck me that, since the Great Whale's reprieve, the politicians of New York and New England and American buyers of HQ power have paid scant attention to the plight of the Cree and their besieged rivers. If the rivers are to be saved, there will have to be a reduction in demand from the American consumer. The outlook for Rupert and the Cree will improve only if Americans threaten to terminate the importation of HQ power unless the company changes its habit of runaway destruction.

Sources

Boyce Richardson, *Strangers Devour the Land*, Vancouver. Douglas & McIntyre, 1991.
www.hydroquebec.com/eastmain1a/en/pdf/eastmain1a_rupert_en.pdf
www.ottertooth.com/Reports/Rupert/News/rupert-surrender.htm

PAUL RUDERSHAUSEN is a fishery biologist living in North Carolina. He has led surveys of trout and salmon populations in remote regions of Idaho and Alaska. He has also led and co-led extended wilderness canoeing expeditions in Quebec.

White Heron Rises Over Blackwater

I wonder
   what it is
      that I will accomplish
         today

if anything
   can be called
      that marvelous word.
         It won't be

my kind of work,
   which is only putting
      words on a page,
         the pencil

haltingly calling up
   the light of the world,
      yet nothing appearing on paper
         half as bright

as the mockingbird's
   verbal hilarity
      in the still unleafed shrub
         in the churchyard—

or the white heron
   rising
      over the swamp
         and the darkness,

his yellow eyes
   and broad wings wearing
      the light of the world
         in the light of the world—

ah yes, I see him.
   He is exactly
      the poem
         I wanted to write

                    —*Mary Oliver*

MARY OLIVER has published more than a dozen volumes of poetry, as well as works of imaginative prose and poetry instruction. Her most recent publication is *New and Selected Poems: Volume Two* (Beacon Press, 2005). In the spring of 2006 Beacon will release a CD, *At Blackwater Pond: Mary Oliver Reads Mary Oliver.* She is a frequent contributor to *Appalachia.*

Karl Limmer

*The Famous Family Boot Continues to Maintain a
Strong Foothold on Mountain Trails*

Doug Mayer and Rebecca Oreskes

Editor's Note: This is the eleventh in a series of profiles of people whose lives have been intricately linked to the mountains of New England. Prepared by New Hampshire residents Doug Mayer of Randolph and Rebecca Oreskes of Milan, these profiles reflect the dynamic life and landscape of the high country, past and present. Mayer and Oreskes welcome suggestions for future profiles, which can be offered by letter to: Appalachia Editor, 5 Joy Street, Boston, MA 02108; or by e-mail to cwoodside@snet.net.

Introduction

For some people, Limmer boots and the White Mountains are inseparable. Many White Mountain hikers wouldn't think of wearing anything other than a sturdy pair of "Limmers," the famed handmade boots from Intervale, New Hampshire. There was a time when Limmer boots were part of an AMC hut or trail crew "uniform," and a first summer paycheck would immediately go to buy a new pair of boots. The first snow rangers in Tuckerman Ravine and members of the Mount Washington volunteer ski patrol in the 1950s all wore Limmer boots. Today, they remain the boot of choice for hardworking trail crews, hut and shelter staff, and other backcountry workers, and because of their unique look, they are recognized immediately by hikers around the world.

The boots are still made by hand in Limmer and Son's Custom Shoemaker's shop in Intervale, just north of North Conway, where Karl Limmer and his cousin, Peter — representing the third generation of Limmer shoemakers — uphold the family tradition.

It's hard to imagine any other outdoor gear for which people have such a strong emotional attachment. Men and women have worn them at their weddings, and some people have been buried in them. There are probably those among us who would have chosen to be born in them, if that had been an option. After AMC hutman Ben Campbell died while hiking in Scotland, his Limmers were nailed to the crew room wall at Lakes of the Clouds Hut. One of Guy Waterman's last wishes was that his Limmer boots be placed in a cairn alongside his son's, deep in the White Mountains.

We interviewed Karl Limmer twice during the summer of 2005. The result will be a two-part interview, with Part II appearing in the next issue. The interview is in his own voice and has been edited only for space and continuity.

Opposite: A rack of consignment boots. Often shoes outlast the original owner.
PHOTO BY NED THERRIEN, NORTH STAR PHOTOGRAPHY

The First Limmer Bootmaker Becomes an Apprentice

This is the family business. My partner and first cousin, Peter, and I are the third generation of our family in New Hampshire to do the craft of hand bootmaking. Our shop has been here since 1951.

Our grandfather, Peter, was one of twelve children. He emigrated from Germany in 1926, at the height of the worldwide Depression. At seventeen, he had been drafted into World War I and sent by the German army to fight on the Russian front. He got captured, was in a prisoner of war camp that 15,000 guys went into and 5,000 came out of. He always said that it wasn't brutality [that caused the deaths], it was starvation. At that time, the Russian people were starving and they couldn't justify feeding their prisoners better than their people.

He finally escaped from an island in the Black Sea and made his way back to Germany through Russia. It was quite a challenge. Everything had broken down, and there were armed factions that didn't necessarily have uniforms that you could see. He says they'd come upon you with their guns on you and they'd say, "Who are you and what's your side?" If you said the wrong thing, they just shot you. I guess he was able to say the right things all the way back home. He had been gone from home for six or seven years. Like a lot of guys that have seen hard times in war, though, he didn't talk about it.

Before he went into the service, my grandfather had mastered his craft as a shoemaker. You did that by middle school. The teachers and your parents decided if you were an academic or if you were a crafts-bound person. They decided for you. It was determined that he should be a shoemaker.

He started by sweeping the floor. He told us he even ended up straightening out the shoe tacks, because they were so frugal they used them over again. It took seven years of living with the shoemaker, under the guild system, for him to become [an official] "master shoemaker." I think it was 1921. We have his master's certificate here on the wall. It was during this time that he met my grandmother. They were married on March 9, 1919.

Along about the time of the Depression, Hitler's name started to come up in politics, and my grandfather saw the handwriting on the wall. He didn't want to be involved in another war. He was definitely not into what the Nazi Party was into. Most of the Bavarians weren't. You see, my family is from southern Germany, the mountainous region. They were laid-back, southern farmers. They were more interested in having a beer and just living life and enjoying their countryside.

So, my grandfather and grandmother landed in Boston in 1926, along with two-year-old Francis (my dad) and four-year-old Peter (my cousin Pete's dad). They had no family in Boston at the time; they didn't have any money, and couldn't speak English. So they naturally gravitated toward Jamaica Plain, which was at that time a German enclave. It had the support system. The language was there, the food was there, and the community helped them out when they first got here. My grandfather did a lot of house painting until he started shoemaking, and my grandmother did a lot of house cleaning.

In the 1940s, World War II came along, and my father and my uncle were both drafted. My father went into the U.S. Army and subsequently into the Tenth Mountain Division. My uncle was in the U.S. Air Force. He stayed stateside during the war. My dad saw action in the Italian Alps at Riva Ridge. In a very short time, his unit sustained some of the highest rate of casualties of any outfit during the war. After the war, many of the guys from the Tenth Mountain Division settled in the Mount Washington valley to promote the infant ski industry.

My dad, Francis, met my mom in 1946 when he was in Boston. My mother was doing seamstress work. She learned to be a seamstress when she was in Germany, and she was there during the war. She saw a lot. It was something that she didn't talk about a lot, just like the soldiers. My mother and father were married in 1950.

Photo of the Limmer family taken in their home in Jamaica Plain circa 1950. From left: Peter Jr., Peter Sr., his wife, Maria, Francis Limmer, and his wife Marielle.

After the war, Uncle Peter went back to visit Germany, where he met his future wife, Marianne. They were married in 1953, and Marianne came to America in 1954. Like my mother, Marianne was in Germany during the war and she saw a lot as well.

Moving to Intervale

During my grandparents' 24 years in Boston, my grandfather started his custom shoe and ski boot business. My grandfather and grandmother made traditional Bavarian-style side-tie shoes. In 1950, my grandfather moved his family up here. We actually have the ad for the land—Pete has it up in front of his workbench. I think it was in the *Boston Globe*, which advertised this place, with 38 acres of land.

I think it was a unanimous decision. Both my dad and my uncle were avid skiers. They were outdoor, athletic types and this area reminded my grandfather of Bavaria, where he was from. He was always a little homesick. One of the things I remember him saying when I was a little kid was, "There were times when we first moved over here that I sat at Revere Beach and looked out over across the ocean and said if I could swim all the way back I would."

When they moved up here, the business was pretty well established. But they weren't making hiking boots yet; they were making dress shoes and ski boots for the MIT and Harvard crowd.

Around 1950, while skiing in Tuckerman Ravine, my dad and uncle met Howard Head, who was working on a prototype metal ski. I think Pete might have one of the first metal skis ever sold, ones his father bought from Howard Head. They're Head skis that are serial number 325. Those are collectors' items, these days. Of course, everybody thought he was crazy to make skis out of metal. But we know how that worked out.

The Birth of the Limmer Hiking Boot

I think the family began making hiking boots right around 1951. I don't know if I could say they had the foresight to know what the outdoor recreation industry would turn into. But it was certainly fortuitous that they ended up here at the time they did, and that they were in this business.

Opposite: Peter Limmer Jr. and Francis Limmer at the shop circa 1970. (Notice the paper boot patterns hanging from the ceiling.) PHOTO COURTESY OF THE LIMMER FAMILY COLLECTION

The business involved ski boots throughout this whole time. They sustained the ski boot business until about 1965, about the time that the plastic ski boots came out. To be honest with you, I think it was somewhat of a relief, because skiers were kind of like complainers, you know? I think they wanted their equipment to be magical and to take the place of physical conditioning! I can remember my dad coming home on Sunday evenings and saying, "All they do is come in and say it hurts me here and it hurts me there."

It was about this time that our hiking boot reputation was starting to grow.

The Next Generation

I didn't really come into the business until about 1967. I graduated from high school in 1970, and for two or three years before that, I would take the Bartlett bus from Kennett High School [in Conway, New Hampshire] and get off at the end of Route 16A or right here on the street and just come in after school. It gave me pocket money.

I did have a choice, though. My mom and dad told me, "If you want to go to college, it's there for you. But if you want to be a shoemaker, that's there for you, too." I'll tell you right now as a hand shoemaker you're never going to go hungry because there'll always be people who can't buy shoes [off the shelf] and you'll always have work. And that's true.

I felt a sense of tradition; a sense of security in the job. Even at that age, I realized it was going to be a good opportunity, that somehow or other I would end up owning a share of the business and have that job security for the long term. My cousin Pete is four years younger than I am, so I'm sure he felt the same way, but he was four years later coming in.

Pete grew up right next to the shop here. Earlier on, our family would celebrate all the holidays together. We were more like brothers than cousins.

My grandmother passed away in 1968, and my grandfather passed away in 1971. It was really hard on my father and my uncle. For years afterwards, there would be customers coming in and asking for them, and each time it was kind of an emotional rub. When you work together like that for your whole life, it's a big loss.

By 1972, I was working pretty much full time. It was difficult to live at home and work with your father. If there was a problem at home, it carried over to work. I think it's natural for your parents to have higher expectations of their own kids than they would others'. So there was a little bit of roughness in the relationship there. But I worked as an employee until 1979, when

I struck out for different scenery, a different life. I lived in Vermont from 1979 to 1985, doing shoemaking there. I realized, though, that it was going to be a lifetime struggle to just get established. I had in mind to have a family and own a home, and I didn't see that coming from the [Vermont work] any time soon. But I befriended the lady who is now my wife, Marie, over in Vermont, and we moved back here in 1985.

The Business Grows

From about 1965 on, we got more and more popular. The word was getting out. There were a few articles. The *Boston Globe* had done an article, and would do more over the years. Each time they do one, the volume of business increases. Our reputation travels by word of mouth. It's slow, but extremely effective.

When 1974 came along, the *Wall Street Journal* did an article on our business. That's when it really exploded. At that time, our backlog was probably six or eight months. Within six months of that article, it was three-and-a-half years [wait for a pair of boots].

We were the first outdoor shop in town. Starting around 1965, you could buy ice axes, crampons, climbing ropes, pitons, and carabiners here. In 1975 or so, my father and my uncle decided to get out of that business. They had

Karl, Francis, and Peter Limmer taking a break from work.

PHOTO COURTESY OF THE LIMMER FAMILY COLLECTION

that lengthy boot backlog, and the old saying is: "Shoemaker, stick to your last." The "last" is the mold that the boots are made over.

During that period, it was always just the family who worked in the business: my grandmother and grandfather, and my mother, aunt, uncle and father, and then my cousin and me. Everybody had a specific job. My grandfather cut the leather for the uppers. My mom and my aunt shared the sewing and the secretarial work.

Back then, the business had low overhead. They didn't have help to pay or insurance benefits to offer. They just kept putting everything into the business. I can remember seeing my dad's paycheck in the early days, and it was something like $65 a week. That was for probably a 50-hour week.

My dad and my uncle were . . . how should I say this? They gave good deals and then complained that they weren't making enough money. Our boots have always been a good value. I can remember more than one customer writing a check to pay for boots and saying they should be more expensive. Now when do people ever buy anything and tell the vendor that they would be willing to pay more? In the retail business, it's a little more justifiable to just add your margin and that's your selling price. Tradespeople, craftspeople tend to be more modest about their craft. They're good craftsmen and not necessarily good businessmen. I would put my father and my uncle into that category.

A Shoemaker's Hazards

In about 1995, I came down with contact dermatitis, due to exposure to the chemicals in the glue. It's a problem I still have. We used to use acetone to wash our hands off at the end of the day, and there were no such things as material safety data sheets. You didn't know what the risk was. My dad was sensitive to it, too. His hands had dried, cracked skin on the palms when he was my age. So after twenty years of fooling around with that stuff, I became sensitive to it. Pete never got sensitive to it. He's the only bootmaker right now. One of our staff, Ken, who does repairs for us—we now consider him a master at boot repairer—he has a problem with that stuff, too, if he's not careful.

Limmers Today

Our boots evolved from White Mountain hiking. My grandfather always made good boots, but when he saw a weak point, he tried to fix it. For

Francis Limmer's skilled hands at work on a new pair of ski boots.

example, how many seams are there? How many inches of stitches are on the boots? Our present-day boots have only a third of the seams that are in the older boots. Fewer seams mean fewer inches of exposed stitches to abrade and fall apart, and better waterproofing.

The climate here is not very different from the climate in Bavaria. What is different is the type of hiking. The mountains in Europe are much newer. This is a theory of mine as to why, say, Italian boots have pointed toes. It's not because Italians have pointed feet. It's because of form following function. You hike in a lot of places, over passes and on trails that are just gravel paths. But when you go to a summit and you're using toe-holds and hand-holds, then you're actually doing rock-climbing. So, that's why you've got a pointier boot. Here, the majority of the distance that you travel is not in that severely abrading stone, but you can still take whole hikes where you're on rock all the way.

The real foundation of our business has always been what we call the core users, the professional outdoor people — the New Hampshire Fish and Game [staff], the AMC trail and hut crews. When people see our boots on those professionals' feet and their ankles are hurting them, they think, "Well, I should buy what the pros buy."

For years, the State of New Hampshire has had Limmer boots — black and shined — as part of their official dress uniform. Their purchasing agent, it's been said, says, "If we fire them, they give back their gun and their boots.'" Over time, people coming up from down country have seen a lot of change between Conway and North Conway. We're proud to be able to say we're one of the only places that you'd still recognize if you haven't been here for twenty years. Our reputation was originally developed and continues today by word of mouth. People believing other people who have the product and aren't being paid to say, "This is a good thing" — it's more effective than paid advertising, where you're trying to create an aura.

I've become very thankful as I get older — maybe because I'm also a little wiser — for what our parents and grandparents did and what we were more or less bequeathed as a blessing to carry on.

End of Part One

Part Two of the interview with Karl Limmer will appear in the Summer/Fall 2006 issue of Appalachia.

DOUG MAYER is trails chair of the Randolph Mountain Club and on the board of directors of the Guy Waterman Alpine Stewardship Fund. He lives in Randolph, New Hampshire, with his partner, Mary Krueger, and their aging Lab, Chloe.

REBECCA ORESKES is Recreation and Wilderness Program Leader for the White Mountain National Forest. She lives in Gorham, New Hampshire, with her husband, Brad Ray.

Mountain Col

We cross a subterranean pond,
high on the mountain ridge
where rivers begin, where
saplings are scarred, denuded
by falling ice and up-ranging

deer. We descend over boulders,
clinging to small branches, roots;
look across the gap to another wall
of rock and scrub. Somewhere deep
in that gray-green mass a trail
slabs to the summit plateau. But first
the col, where sky on sunny days
unfolds its wings and birds soar through—

not today. Clouds
boil up from the notch toward
the valley to the west, tepid
rain dashes snow to slush. We

pause, wriggle boots in icy mush,
breathe. Ahead lies a warming
scramble, a summit spun
in whirlpools, a caress of air.

—Parker Towle

Employed by the Dartmouth-Hitchcock Clinic, PARKER TOWLE practices neurology
in the north country of New Hampshire. He is also on the faculty of the Frost Festival
of Poetry, in Franconia, New Hampshire, and he is an associate editor at *The Worcester
Review*. Recent poems have appeared in *Blueline*, *Common Ground Review*, *Compass
Rose*, and *The Cape Rock*.

Last Light Fading

Another Season on the Appalachian Trail

By Ryan J. Harvey

PHOTO BY TONY MARPLE, COURTESY OF AMC PHOTO LIBRARY

A T THE WILL OF THE WIND, I SWAY HIGH ABOVE THE TREETOPS. I clench tightly onto the weathered trunk of the balsam fir, balancing on a single branch. The roots rock with the wind. Covering the scarred bedrock, the forest floor of peat and sphagnum rises and falls, remaining intact only by the balsams' shallow root systems. The howling winds indicate a shifting weather front coming in from northwest. I have not received a weather forecast, but from experience in the mountains I am certain. Between the gusts of wind, I take advantage of the stillness and snap a few pictures of the dynamic landscape spread before me. The ridgeline of Saddle Ball Mountain descends below, while the summit of Mount Greylock rises from the saddle, its western flanks plummeting into the glacial basin of the Hopper. Not a cloud can be seen. The sky is flushed by the roaring winds. Northward, the Green Mountains disappear into the horizon, and a late summer's alpenglow casts a reddish hue across the Greylock Massif. Its summit basks in the light — the last land touched by the day.

It is my final shift on the Appalachian Trail for the season. More important, it is my last Greylock shift and possibly even my last ridgerunner season. I have felt honored to be one of the few paid AT backcountry rangers — called the ridgerunners — and to work with such a dedicated group of passionate volunteers. Sunsets, however, don't pay college loans, and I might soon need to find more lucrative employment.

My destination tonight is the Mark Noepel Shelter, one of my favorites, nestled amongst the dark boreal forest on the eastern slope of the mountain. But Greylock lures me towards its summit. Drawn by the moment, I begin to pack up and prepare for an exposed bivouac at the top. Despite the howling winds above, the forest itself remains silent as the lingering light of dusk guides me.

I reach the summit just as the sun sheds its last ray over the Taconics. Taking advantage of the scattered post-sunset glow, I wander through the grass and sedge meadows of the summit searching for a place to hunker down for the night. Amidst the meadows and rock outcroppings, I find an attractive bivy ledge with a sweeping view to the east where the sun will soon kiss the summit again. My headboard is exposed bedrock crowned with steeplebush. A flat rock, possible debris from the last ice age, lies at my feet. To the unknowing, the draping meadows follow the fall line down to the cripplebush

Opposite: Carter Dome, New Hampshire (elevation 4,832). One of many beautiful mountains draped in snow and ice on the Appalachian Trail.

below, where the forest will again flourish. The mountain plummets precariously beneath my snug bivouac, forming the headwall of the great 1990 landslide. The landslide abruptly drops into a fan of deposited scree and talus. It was just last winter that my climbing partner and I made the first ascent up its iced face. We made our way up an attractive rock and ice route following a prominent gully out and over the intimidating "balcony," an exposed slab interrupted by a small headwall. My bivouac for the night is on the spot where we celebrated our success.

With little space to work, I set up my makeshift bivouac. It has become dark, but the stars are bright in the absence of a moon. I lie down to search for the Milky Way, and Mars rises above me. On this night, Mars is the closest it's been to Earth for a few thousand years. And at this moment, I am a little closer to it than many.

The stunted subalpine forests that surround me are a testament to the unforgiving mountain weather. Dictated by the mountain's microclimate, these forests persist in the most exposed areas of the mountain. The krummholtz of spruce and fir come in various unique forms shaped by the desiccating winds. Flag trees tower above the low cripplebush, with dieback indicating the direction of the prevailing winds, which originate primarily from the west. Other trees resemble broomsticks with live branches appearing only at the top of bare trunks. Their crowns have grown above the abrasion zone of the windblown ice. These sub-alpine species are evolutionarily adapted to the harsh mountain climate. I myself am not.

The cold front, increasingly strong and steady, moves in throughout the night. In the shelter of the leeward slope of the mountain, I listen to the winds howl on the exposed summit above. I watch the temperature fall until it reaches the night's low in the high 30s (Fahrenheit). I quickly realized my 25-degree sleeping bag is no longer as warm as the day I bought it. It has lost much of its loft and, with it, the warmth from the past three seasons on the trail. This night would be the true test of my bivy system—my sleeping pad and sleeping bag inserted into my single-wall tent, and my head hanging out the door opening. My body warmth begins to create condensation on the inside of the thin nylon of my tent. To keep from getting wet, I rustle my rain fly over my bivouac and stake it down from the wind. At this point, wearing all the layers of clothing I packed, I hunker down into a mountaineer's slumber.

I wake before the first light of day and watch the morning sun rise up and over the high Berkshire Plateau, cast its first light upon the summit, and slowly descend the mountain to enlighten the valleys below. The northerly cold front has finally arrived, and the winds have subsided.

I share the early morning with a white-throated sparrow welcoming the new day with its nostalgic song; old sam peabody, peabody, peabody. My favorite birdsong, it exemplifies these lofty remnants of the post-glacial era. I know I have reached the higher ground of the Northeast when the white-throated sparrow welcomes me into the alpine landscape.

I warmed my hands preparing the morning's breakfast. Gazing out and over the awakening mountains, I feel an overwhelming sense of contentment and respect. I have experienced many awesome moments in the mountains, but every sunrise is a new spiritual moment.

John Muir has written, "Climb the mountains and get their good tidings. Nature's peace will flow into you as sunshine flows into trees. The winds will blow their own freshness into you." The mountains have become my cathedrals, and I hope always to return for their good tidings.

Ryan J. Harvey lives in Wentworth, New Hampshire, with the Appalachian Trail at his doorstep. He served as a ridgerunner on the Appalachian Trail for three seasons and as a winter weather observer for the Mount Washington Observatory. Currently, he works for the U.S. Forest Service in the White Mountain National Forest.

Letters

Dear Editor,

I enjoy *Appalachia* so much! And your delightful piece about Isle au Haut reminded me that my grandparents were from Maine and had sometimes spoken of "Eel-uh-hoe." I don't know if they'd ever been there or just knew people who had.

I also note that I recently reread, with pleasure, a book on my shelves, *Here on the Island*, by Charles Pratt (Harper and Row, New York, 1974.) You may well know of it.

I'm a happy life member of AMC. Most of my involvement has been open-boat whitewater canoeing.

With thanks for much good reading.

— *Charles B. Woodbury*
Lexington, Massachusetts

Dear Editor,

The [Spring/Summer] issue of *Appalachia* arrived at this outpost of civilization, and I dropped everything to read that issue, as I am an old Katahdin lover. Many years ago, I lived in Rhode Island, and I chaired the Narragansett AMC Chapter and did rock work for many years.

In younger days, there were four of us who formed our own mountain club and went by the name of Palpitating Pups. We made trips winter and summer, though never all of us together—usually only three on each trip.

In 1932, we were in Maine, at Chimney Pond on Katahdin. It was our second expedition to that mountain. Roy Dudley, the game warden in residence, had cut a tree to use as a flagpole. On July 23, we took the Parsons Trail to the foot of Saddle Slide, picked up the tree, and carried it back to Chimney Pond. We took the bark off, and after Roy had fixed a small pulley, we set the pole in place.

After that trip, at the usual reading of our club log, we pooled our funds (Depression days were over, but money was still tight) and bought a gold ball, which we sent to Roy and friends. For some years after, they told us the pole and ball were still in place.

Roy had a young son, about ten in 1932. He offered to split some wood for us to use in the pit for cooking. After watching him split the first piece, though, we suggested he not do any more. We had watched him put the short log on the ground, and with his bare feet holding the log in place, swing a full-size axe down between his feet. He would have preferred to continue, but we politely said, "No."

A great issue. Keep the faith!

— Richmond A. Day
Grand Forks, North Dakota

Dear Editor,

The Summer/Fall 2005 issue of *Appalachia*, including my profile of Baxter State Park director Buzz Caverly, emerged the same week Buzz retired from his career-long job, the one he had told me he wasn't ready to leave any time soon. When I spent a day in the park with Buzz and his wife, Jan, in October 2004, he said that he felt his career was half over, even though he had reached age 65. That is why my article makes the claim that he had no plans to retire. Eight months later, in June 2005, he surprised his staff—and me—by changing his mind. By the end of that month, he had left "the best job in state government."

In late July, I spent five days backpacking in Baxter. Rangers and gate keepers told me that they had been surprised, and yet not entirely surprised, at Caverly's quick and decisive move to retire.

"My plan was to work until I was 70," Caverly told me when I called his house in Corinth, Maine. But practical and health considerations came up suddenly. "I decided it would be good for the park if I moved on."

He said that he and his wife (who herself worked long years at Baxter) have done some traveling, but that they also are enjoying the novelty of staying put in their house on ten acres, which he calls a mini–Baxter State Park. He admitted that he misses the real Baxter. "There's not a day that goes by when I don't think about going up there and taking care of something," he said. "And then I remember it's not my responsibility any more."

Buzz told me he and Jan want to thank the many associates and friends they met through Baxter State Park. "We wish all of those people the very best of luck and 'Happy trails' forever."

— Christine Woodside
Deep River, Connecticut

Accidents

THERE WERE NO FATALITIES REPORTED IN THE WHITE MOUNTAINS during the past winter hiking season, welcome news after the five fatalities observed last winter. In spite of the very icy conditions on all trails during the first half of winter, there was only one fall requiring rescue; I presume that the severity of the icing persuaded most hikers to use some kind of traction device.

Two of the accidents, both involving climbers, illustrate the classic result of bad decisions. On the other hand, the accident on Wildcat Slide is a rare example of a winter accident in which errors of judgment played no role. Nevertheless, as the second potentially fatal accident on that slide in less than a decade, it forces winter hikers to give serious thought to how to deal with that slide. Keith Sullivan was kind enough to send me details of his approach to crossing that slide safely. Others may prefer to use another route, but I fear that many will continue to cross it unprotected.

Reports of accidents on the east slopes of Mount Washington (Cutler River Drainage) are taken from the website (www.tuckerman.org) maintained by the U.S. Forest Service, which is responsible for rescues in that area. I thank Brad Ray for bringing that excellent site to my attention. Most of the other reports are from the files of the New Hampshire Fish and Game Department, the state agency charged with responsibility for overseeing searches and rescues within the rest of the state. When other sources are used they are explicitly named. It is important to note that www.tuckerman.org website does not use names, which is why you will find them missing from those accounts.

The Fish and Game Department and the White Mountain National Forest have jointly developed an excellent web site with safety information for hikers at www.hikesafe.com, and I recommend you visit it if you have not already done so.

Avalanche in Huntington Ravine

(From a posting by Chris Joosen, Lead Snow Ranger, on the www.tuckerman. org website.)

On January 7, 2005, A and R (this website does not provide names) planned to climb North Gully in Huntington Ravine after spending the night at the Harvard Cabin. The previous day, they had climbed O'Dell's Gully, which had gone very well. Brian Johnston, USFS Snow Ranger, passed the Harvard Cabin at around 6:50 A.M. When he heard the pair planned to climb North Gully, Johnston said he didn't recommend climbing in the ravine that day because of the avalanche danger. They discussed how they might approach their intended route without being in the runout of avalanche paths. Because of their climb the day before, they knew the overhanging tree Johnston referred to as a reference. At this location, he said, the safest route would be to take a hard right up into the talus, but he again mentioned that he could not recommend climbing in the ravine. They had no avalanche gear and told me later that they typically rented a probe, shovel, and beacon when the avalanche danger was "Considerable" or "High."

Although North Gully was rated a "Considerable" danger that day, it was the gully of lowest concern compared to the other avalanche areas in Huntington Ravine. They determined to at least go up and take a look.

A and R left the Harvard cabin at 8:15 A.M. and spent more than an hour getting into the base of the Fan in Huntington. They went far beyond the downed tree Johnston had indicated as a turning point and started moving straight up the center of the Fan. They could not see the gullies due to blowing snow, and they estimated there was 100- to 150-feet visibility. They went uphill an estimated 100 feet before stopping to adjust their clothing. A was in front. Bending over, he removed his gloves to adjust his balaclava. He said later that he thought to himself, "'Boy this isn't a good place to be stopping." At just that moment, an avalanche hit him.

A estimated he had slid only 40 feet, but he was completely buried. As the debris slowed to a stop, his head and feet were facing up. He frantically punched his arms up in front of his face and thrashed to free himself. He could feel the snow already setting around him, but within 15 seconds he was fairly free.

R had slid about 55 feet and was about 15 feet below A. He was buried to his waist. The air was so obscured that he could not see his friend above him. R felt he was at the terminal toe of the debris, which averaged 4 to 5 feet in depth.

They had lost A's gloves and two mountaineering axes but spent no time looking for them, moving as quickly as they could to get out of the ravine. The only injury was a scrape and some bruising on A's right shin.

Comment: Lead Snow Ranger Chris Joosen commented that the two climbers should have recognized this as a "no-go" situation, given the avalanche danger, the weather forecast, and the early warning from Johnston. Add minimal visibility to the avalanche danger, and the decision to proceed seems even less rational. To proceed without avalanche gear amounts, in my opinion, to reckless behavior. The snow ranger did his best to dissuade them from proceeding, but then could do no more than advise them of the least dangerous way of doing so and letting them make their own decision. He did not have the authority to stop them, and those of us who cherish the "freedom on the hills" feel that that is indeed the right approach. The fact that they didn't even take the ranger's advice makes their situation seem even more irresponsible. These two had traveled a long distance to go climbing, so they seemed determined to climb at all costs. This is the worst possible attitude with which to approach the mountains, particularly in winter. When conditions change, plans must be reevaluated.

Climbers Spend a Cold Night Above Huntington Ravine

(From a posting on the www.tuckerman.org website.)

On January 24, 2005, D.M. and S.S. (this website does not provide names) planned to climb Damnation Gully after spending the night at the Harvard Cabin. D.M. had climbed the route previously, but it was to be S.S.'s first ice climb. They left the cabin shortly before 11:00 A.M. and started their climb sometime around noon. According to D.M., they encountered a lot of wet and poor ice and bad belay stations. They had also underestimated the length of the gully, so their descent was long and slow. They decided not to rappel, since S.S. had never done so, and they reached the top of the gully near dusk. When they topped out, they encountered high west-northwest winds, which prevented them from making their way around to the Escape Hatch. They tried to find a descent route towards Nelson Crag, but due to the winds and poor visibility, they turned back toward Huntington and found a sheltered spot where they hunkered down for the evening.

The Harvard Mountaineering Club (HMC) caretaker contacted the Forest Service at 10:00 P.M. to report that the pair was overdue from their climb. Winds at that time were reported to be gusting to 70 mph, and the temperature was minus 6 degrees Fahrenheit. The HMC and AMC caretakers went into Huntington between 1:00 and 2:00 A.M., yelling into the darkness and looking for lights. When they did not find anything, rescue teams from Mountain Rescue Service (MRS) and Androscoggin Valley Search and Rescue (AVSAR) were asked to be ready at first light to search for the pair.

One team of rescuers was transported up the Auto Road in the Mount Washington State Park snowcat to begin looking above Huntington Ravine from the Alpine Garden and Huntington Ravine trails. Other teams were transported up to the Lion Head Trail and into Huntington Ravine. At dawn, the pair again tried to make their way to the Escape Hatch. Temperatures had dropped to minus 17 degrees Fahrenheit, and winds were about 80 mph with higher gusts. At times, rescuers dropped to their hands and knees to protect themselves from the wind. Fog and blowing snow made visibility difficult. As the fog lifted, D.M. & S.S. were spotted near the top of Central Gully. Rescuers reached them around 8:30 A.M., gave them food and water, and assisted them to the Auto Road and the waiting snowcat. They were suffering from frostbite and hypothermia. At the base of the Auto Road, the two were transferred to a waiting ambulance and taken to Androscoggin Valley Hospital.

Comment: This is an example of several errors of judgment that, in combination, could have led to serious injury or even death. The first error was choosing Mount Washington as the site of S.S.'s first ice climb. A climbing area close to a road, where the pair would have been free to concentrate on the technical aspects without having to deal with the notorious Mount Washington weather, would have been much more suitable. Furthermore, doing a serious climb without knowing how to rappel down is unwise. It makes it impossible to abort the climb due to lateness or deteriorating conditions. It also forced the pair to descend by an exposed route in bad weather after reaching the top of the climb.

The accident report suggests that the forecast was for bad weather. The two climbers had come from Connecticut, and as with the two friends involved in the accident outlined above, climbers who come long distances are often reluctant to adjust their plans to the conditions.

Even though the late start did not directly contribute to the problems, there is no justification for starting a climb at 11:00 A.M. at a time of the year when the sun sets at about 4:30 It is critically important to get an early start.

I believe that all of the errors are due to the same underlying cause: considering this as a technical climb rather than as a mountaineering expedition. In Classic Backcountry Skiing, David Goodman writes, "Backcountry skiing is really just winter mountaineering on skis — hence the term ski mountaineering, which aptly describes most of the ski tours in this book. To travel safely in the winter wilderness, skiers need good mountaineering skills." The same clearly applies to those climbers who choose to climb far from roads. Unfortunately, many of those who ski or climb on the eastern slopes of Mount Washington concentrate on the technical aspects of their trip, largely ignoring the all-important mountaineering aspects. Some end up having cause to regret it.

This rescue, which took 32 people and ten hours to complete, was an outstanding example of teamwork. If not for the skill and organization of the local search and rescue community, the result could well have been different.

Hiker Falls Down Wildcat Slide

(Facts from a posting by David W. Benham, a member of the victim's group, on the Maine Outdoor Adventure Club's website www.moac.org, and from Marjorie LaPan, the leader of the AMC group that participated in the rescue.)

On January 8, 2005, Carl N. was climbing Wildcat A from Carter Notch, with the intention of going over the ridge to Wildcat D and descending by the ski slopes (the standard winter approach). He was with five companions and his dog. Carl and some of his companions had been on this trail before in winter conditions, so they knew what was ahead.

Partway up this steep trail, there is a short, 20- to 25-foot-wide open slide that one must cross horizontally to pick up the trail on the other side. The slide runs steeply down the mountain several hundred feet and disappears below into the woods. Carl N. snagged his crampon while crossing, stumbled, and fell down the slide, pulling his dog with him. One of his companions immediately descended through the woods parallel to the slide and found him lying on the ground, conscious but unable to move. Others immediately went to the hut to ask for help. Two other groups of hikers (a New Hampshire Chapter AMC group and a non-AMC group from New York) were nearby, and they included several physicians, one of whom was an orthopedic surgeon. In addition, another hiker had training and experience in ski patrol rescue. They quickly got his leg splinted, put him in a sleeping bag and bivy sack, and gave him warm fluids. The Carter Notch hutmaster soon arrived and took charge of the rescue. He brought a sled into which the victim was put, and the evacuation started.

The fall had occurred around noon, and by 2:00 P.M. they were ready to start lowering him through the woods down the mountain. Some sections were steep, and over those sections the hutmaster set up a belay line to lower the sled. Eventually, they reached the 19-mile Brook Trail, and here it was decided that the New York group, which was staying at the hut, was not needed for the rest of the rescue. Pulling a sled downhill on a trail does not require much manpower. By 6:00 P.M., they had gotten him to the road, where an ambulance was waiting. He was taken to a hospital and treated for multiple fractures. His dog, who had slid all the way with him, was not injured.

Comment: Most serious winter accidents are due to errors of judgment, but this one is an exception. This mishap was dealt with in an exemplary way, thanks to the knowledge and preparedness of many of those involved.

On the other hand, there is no doubt that the victim also benefited from luck. The two other groups that were close by provided the essential manpower for a self-rescue, saving much time and greatly decreasing the risk of hypothermia in both the victim and his companions. The orthopedic surgeon was obviously better qualified to splint multiple fractures than a layperson, even one with first-aid training, and he substantially reduced the victim's pain. The hiker with ski patrol experience knew how to handle a rescue sled. The availability of a sleeping bag and bivy sack plus ample warm fluids prevented hypothermia.

This is the second serious accident on that slide in less than a decade. In January 1998 a hiker crossing the slide lost a crampon and fell several hundred feet. This slide is one of the few places in our generally gentle mountains (in terms of terrain, not weather) where a simple slip will lead to a serious, potentially fatal fall. The classic approach to the Wildcats in winter is a traverse, crossing the slide on the way up to the "A" peak, then going over the ridge to the gondola station and down by the ski slopes. It is also possible to do a round trip, going both up and down the ski slopes. This adds only about 1.5 miles, but it does mean crossing the ridge, with its innumerable ups and downs, twice. In compensation, it avoids the very steep climb from Carter Notch to the "A" peak. There is no doubt in my mind that this is the safest approach, but it is not widely used. Perhaps after this second accident, it will be used more often.

It is best to avoid going over the Wildcats in icy conditions. I have crossed that slide once in winter, with snow rather than ice on the trail, and under those conditions it seems almost totally innocuous. Unfortunately it is often difficult to predict conditions before getting on the trail, and few winter hikers would be likely to turn around on finding the slide icy.

Some hikers, usually those with mountaineering experience, set up a fixed line to cross that slide. This is a safe strategy if used by knowledgeable people, but few hikers have either the equipment or the experience to use it safely. As former "Accidents" editor Gene Daniell wrote in his comment on the 1998 accident, "Perhaps the main reason such a rope is not carried more frequently is that we tend to maintain a strict dichotomy between technical and nontechnical climbing, and do not consider ways in which a rope could contribute to safety in some hazardous conditions on nontechnical trips. It is a mindset we would all do well to challenge."

Keith Sullivan, a New Hampshire Chapter trip leader and the informal leader of the group involved in the 1998 accident, kindly sent me the following description of how he now deals with the slide crossing: "Traverse the slide with a rope (8 mm or greater). You'll need 70 to 80 feet of rope to tie off on each side of the slide. The rope will end up perpendicular to the slope and be pulled rather tight. The party members don't need harnesses; enough 1-inch webbing to tie securely around their waists will do the trick, along with a couple of carabiners attached to each end of a 3-foot length of webbing or accessory cord (5 mm would be strong enough). Attach one carabiner to your waist webbing, clip the other into the traverse line and walk across the slide protected from a fall. One climber will need to belay another across the slide to attach and remove the rope when setting up the traverse line."

Non-Fatal Heart Attack in Tuckerman Ravine

(From a posting on the www.tuckerman.org website.)

On April 15, 2005, USFS Snow Rangers were informed of a 69-year-old male having chest pains and shortness of breath on the Tuckerman Ravine Trail below Hermit Lake (this website does not provide names). A ranger responded immediately, calling for a snowcat to transport the victim to Pinkham Notch and for an ambulance to meet the party there. The ranger administered oxygen before the transport to Pinkham. Within 45 minutes of the reporting of the accident, the patient was in an ambulance.

Comment: As hikers continue to head for the mountains as they age, heart attacks have become a regular feature of the summer accidents pages. Now, for the second year in a row, we have seen heart attacks in winter.

Clearly, aging hikers — like myself — should take the time for regular medical checkups and stay fit all year-round. Aside from those and other regular precautions appropriate to the season and the weather, we go to the mountains knowing we are assuming a bit more risk as we age.

In Separate Incidents, Two Hikers Get Lost Along Zealand Road

On December 25, 2005, Howard R., 50, planned to hike along Zealand Road to Wildlife Pond. At the pond, about 1:30 P.M., he asked another hiker how to get back to the parking lot and was advised to take a right at the end of Wildlife Pond Trail. He took the right up the snowmobile trail that leads to Mount Tom. After some time, he lost the trail and tried to head south to reach the parking lot. He was reported overdue, and was located approximately 4 miles from Zealand Road around midnight by rescuers who had followed his tracks in the snow. He had neither a map nor a compass with him.

On February 24, 2005, Alexander S., 14, was hiking along Zealand Road with his mother, Dianne A. and his younger sister Eloise S. (no age given for the latter two). Alexander requested permission to go ahead, claiming to know the way. He took a wrong turn at the first junction, and followed Snowmobile Corridor 11 back to Rt. 3 in Carroll, where he was found. The rest of his group continued to Zealand Hut, assuming that he was ahead of them. Rescuers took him to the AMC Highland Center, and made radio contact with his mother at the hut. Alexander spent the night at Highland Center, his mother and sister stayed at the hut. They walked out next morning and picked Alexander up at the center.

Comment: Zealand Road is flat, widely used, and close to "civilization," so it seems very unthreatening. Nevertheless, people get lost in that area every year. Unfortunately, Howard R. attempted to go south to the parking lot, which in fact is to the north! As soon as Howard found Zealand Road difficult to follow, he should have turned around. A map and a compass would obviously have helped, but in this area, many maps do not show the snowmobile trails.

The HikeSafe website is unambiguous in its disapproval of splitting groups. The third item of its Hiker Responsibility Code states: "When you start as a group, hike as a group, end as a group. Pace your hike to the slowest person." There is no doubt that always heeding this advice would prevent all the "separated hiker" accidents, but I feel that it ignores the real-life dynamics of hiking in a group whose members hike at different speeds. On the other hand, it is good to follow this advice in the winter season, since the risk of separation can be much greater in cold conditions. It seems hard to get lost on Zealand Road, especially for someone who allegedly "knows the way." When hiking alone, I often have to force myself to concentrate fully on the trail, not let my thoughts wander, and not take anything for granted.

Hiker Slips on Ice on Lincoln Woods Trail

On January 2, 2005, Thomas O'T., 32, was hiking on the Lincoln Woods trail when he slipped on a patch of ice. He felt sharp pain in his left ankle and heard a noise. Two of his companions walked out to seek help, while one stayed with him. He was evacuated by ATV.

Comment: The earlier part of this past winter witnessed a remarkable snow drought, which led to icy trails. Almost every time I was on the Lincoln Woods Trail (either at the start of a real hike, or just going there for a walk), the trail was a river of ice. Most hikers must have used crampons (or other traction devices, such as StabilIcers) extensively, which accounts for the fact that this is the only accident of its kind reported.

Hiker Collision on Mount Washington

(From a posting on the www.tuckerman.org website.)

Three hikers sustained minor injuries on the eastern slopes of Mount Washington (two in Tuckerman Ravine, the third on the winter Lion Head route), and were helped to Pinkham by snow rangers. One of these is particularly interesting:

On March 19, 2005, a hiker was descending the Lion Head winter route when another hiker fell and slid into him. This caused the victim to fall and twist his left knee. He was able to make his way to Hermit Lake where he was aided by the Mount Washington Volunteer Ski Patrol. He was transported to Pinkham via snowmobile by a USFS snow ranger.

Comment: The winter Lion's Head route is steep, usually packed hard, and often crowded. It is easy to slip on it, and the crowding greatly increases the risk of a collision. I am surprised that such accidents are not more frequent.

Hiker Falls into Snow Hole

On March 18, 2005, Stephen M., 56, was descending the Ammonoosuc Ravine Trail with an unnamed companion when they lost the trail around treeline. They followed a GPS bearing toward Gem Pool, and while hiking along a brook drainage, Stephen fell through the snow into a hole 7 feet deep and 4 feet wide. He was initially unable to get out, and his companion called for assistance. Eventually, however, he was able to get out, and their would-be rescuer found them at the trailhead. Both appeared prepared for winter conditions.

Comment: This accident report is brief, which is usual when no real rescue is involved, so many questions are unanswered. Since the trail is fairly close to the stream, I am assuming the two hikers found it soon after Stephen M. extricated himself from the hole.

Last winter, in a report on an incident in which a GPS was available but not used to its full potential, I wrote: "The main function of a GPS is to prevent its owner from getting lost, not to rescue him or her *after* getting lost. For that, some preparation before the trip is essential. At a minimum, waypoints should be recorded for the major landmarks on the trail. . . ." This is the first accident I have come across in which a GPS was indeed used that way. Gem Pool is about a mile from treeline, but the trail goes basically in a straight line toward the pool, and since it is close to the stream much of the way, these hikers had an excellent chance of finding it.

While the GPS was used appropriately, I question the use of the cell phone before the pair had made a serious attempt at dealing with the problem themselves. In "The Celling of the Backcountry" (published in the December 1997 *Appalachia*) Sandy Stott writes:

> . . . it seems that ease of communication creates a risk of too-quick reaction, and this is only heightened when one considers how most of us respond to the sight and sound of someone in pain. We rush to help. In the backcountry such rushing may unleash an unneeded rescue effort, and it may keep people from the self-reliance of rescuing themselves.

In this case, only one rescuer was dispatched, but Stott's advice is good to remember.

Injured Hiker on Mount Chocorua

Editor's Note: Information about this accident was taken directly from one of the parties involved. The accident was not reported to Fish and Game, because group members managed a successful self-rescue. Jerry K. is an orthopedic surgeon.

On February 13, Jerry K. was climbing Mount Chocorua on the Champney Falls Trail with his sons, Colin (16) and Graham (15), and an adult friend, Kai T. The temperature was in the 20s, and wind on the top about 30 mph from the northwest. There was excellent snow cover, and the trail was well packed. The bare top was ice, rock, and snow. Champney Falls Trail joins the Liberty Trail and ascends the summit cone on the southwest aspect. About 40 yards before that junction, Colin and Graham began leading the group directly up the northwest aspect of the summit cone. Using crampons and ice axe, Graham started up, with Colin following. In the deep snow, Colin was about 10 feet above the regular trail, with his left knee flexed more than 90 degrees and was pushing very hard on an exposed piece of rock, when he twisted his knee. He could not move and screamed for help. Jerry called for Graham to drop back to Colin and Jerry climbed up. After extricating Colin's leg from the snow, Jerry and Graham slid Colin down to the regular trail. Colin had been lightly dressed during the uphill exertion, so they got him into his extra fleece layer and wind jacket with hood and heavy gloves. Since the knee appeared stable, Jerry elected to splint it, using a SAM splint, a hiking pole, and triangular bandages from the first-aid kit to secure the splint. It was painful, but the leg could bear some weight. Colin started to walk out with his arm over Jerry's shoulder, using a hiking pole as a cane on the other side.

The evacuation across the open top of Chocorua over the Sister was difficult and slow. When Colin had descended to treeline and was out of the wind, the splint was removed, because it was not actually providing comfort. Progress on the packed trail was easier but still very slow. The group elected to use Graham's snowboard, which was in the car at the trailhead, to slide Colin out. Graham and Kai descended rapidly to get the snowboard, while Jerry continued down with Colin. Colin's knee began to feel more comfortable, and he made slightly faster progress. Kai and Graham rejoined Colin and Jerry between the switchbacks and the top of the loop trail to the falls. Colin sat on the snowboard and Kai pulled him using a small length of rope. They passed jumper cables from the car around Colin's torso. Following the snowboard, Jerry held the cables like reins to slow the descent on steeper segments. Progress was quite fast with this set-up. About half an hour from the parking lot, the party was joined by another hiker, who had hurried up from the lot with a plastic sled. Colin was loaded onto the sled for the rest of the evacuation, which ended about 4:00 P.M.

Comment: The group declined to use the cell phone they were carrying and chose to rely on themselves to carry out the evacuation. Relying on a cell phone as your means of rescue is risky, since cell phone service is often not available in remote areas and, even in the best circumstances, organizing a rescue takes a substantial amount of time. Staying put on the northwest aspect of the summit cone for several hours would have been dangerous, given the wind exposure and the cold. Self-rescue got the group out of the exposure and kept them warm, since they were moving.

Several issues made this self-rescue smooth. First, each hiker in the group had extra warm clothing that helped prevent hypothermia in the victim. Second, the group carried appropriate first-aid materials. Third, the group had plenty of food and water. Fourth, the group was trained in dealing with emergency situations: Jerry had been trained as a Wilderness First Responder and had completed Mountain Leadership School with the AMC. Wilderness First Aid courses take only a weekend and are recommended to those who do outdoor recreation. Fifth, a fellow hiker was kind enough to offer help.

Unprovoked Grizzly Attack in Alaska

Editor's Note: The following information was taken from an article written by Tom Kizzia, a reporter for the Anchorage Daily News, *and published by the* News *on June 27, 2005. It was sent to* Appalachia *by contributing editor Jeff Fair, who lives in Palmer, Alaska. We include it here, without additional comment, as a complement to "In Grizzly Country" in this issue.*

On Saturday, June 26, Rich and Kathy Huffman, an Anchorage attorney and his wife, a retired schoolteacher, were found to have been killed in their tent while camping along the Hulahula River in the Arctic National Wildlife Refuge. The two were characterized as "cautious veterans of the Alaska wilderness," whose camp was a model of grizzly-conscious planning and implementation. Fish and Game officials said they had stored their food in bear-proof containers far from their tent.

Fish and Game spokesman Bruce Bartley said he believed this to be a predatory attack, a very rare event, particularly since the bear was a healthy male. A gun was found in the camp, but it had not been fired. The 300-pound bear attacked the Huffmans in their sleeping bags and tore at their bodies but did not completely devour them. The grizzly was later tracked and killed by North Slope Borough Search and Rescue officials, who flew by helicopter to the scene.

The ransacked campsite was spotted by someone passing in a river raft, according to North Slope police. The passerby tried to approach the camp but was chased away by the bear. He reported the scene to police.

The attack occurred in the heart of the refuge's coastal plain, a tundra region. The Hulahula runs from the Romanzof Mountains north across the coastal plain to the Beaufort Sea. Kaktovik, an Inupiat village of about 300 residents, is the only community in the area.

Bartley said about six people per year are injured by bear attacks in Alaska, two-thirds of them hunters who surprise bears in the wilderness. Every other year, on average, someone is killed, usually by a brown bear, he said. Usually the bear is defending itself after being surprised, or protecting its young or a fresh kill. "If bears wanted to eat you, they would. We'd lose one a day," said Bartley.

On the other hand, hundreds of bears are killed every year by people defending life or property. Such killings always increase after a widely publicized killing by a bear, said Bartley.

—*Mohamed Ellozy*
"Accidents" Editor

Fisher

Streaks across the road ahead
into the winter trees,
a vivid, long-tailed shadow
against the frozen snow.

Belief is irrelevant.
The world is,
and I am in it.

This fierce weasel
does not mean anything, is not
either less or more

than the snowshoe hare,
than the blood
on its warm gums.

—Daniel Lusk

DANIEL LUSK's poems have appeared in *New Letters*, *North Dakota Quarterly*, *Nimrod*, and *Oberon*. Others have appeared in *Poetry*, *American Poetry Review*, *The North American Review*, and dozens of other literary reviews. His most recent collection of poems is *Kissing the Ground: New & Selected Poems* (Onion River, 1999).

Alpina

*A Semi-Annual Review of Mountaineering
in the Greater Ranges*

China and Tibet

For many years, permission for foreigners to climb in this huge area was severely restricted, requiring patient negotiations sometimes taking years. The Japanese were skilled at this and therefore dominated foreign climbing—particularly in more remote areas. More recently, there was a marked loosening and speeding up of the permit process, sometimes expedited by more-or-less self-appointed brokers and agents.

Now, there has been a slight reversal, making it again difficult for westerners to set up firm arrangements to climb in the more remote mountain areas of eastern Tibet and southern China. The reversal does not seem to be the result of a concerted effort to discourage the expansion of foreign mountaineering; rather, it appears to be caused by uncertainties about the scope and power of the various new and relatively inexperienced Chinese mountaineering associations, coupled with an attempt to rein in some of the more reckless efforts of quasi-official or unofficial agents and brokers. Whatever the cause, some Western expeditions have had their permits invalidated at the last minute. While they have often been able to arrange for alternative goals, these have typically been less desirable, difficult to reach, or even hard to locate.

The wider interest in these areas by Western climbers is partly traceable to the efforts of the Japanese mountain explorer, Tamotsu Nakamura. Nakamura's articles and, especially, his handsome photos, published in *Japanese Alpine News* and the 2003 *American Alpine Journal*, brought these beautiful mountains to widespread attention. One result was the ascent of **Siguniang** (6,250 m) in Szechuan by Americans Tim Boelter and Jon Otto with Chinese Ma Yihua on November 17, 2004. Although this ascent of the mountain was the fifth overall, it was the first by a Chinese and was repeated on the next day by three more Chinese mountaineers from the same expedition. This cooperative effort by the Americans is similar to the arrangements that Japanese expeditions have long used to facilitate access to Chinese mountains.

Of course, all American efforts in Chinese mountains do not derive from Nakamura's articles. For example, Charlie Fowler made a number of first ascents in remote areas, and much earlier, in 1932, Dick Burdsall and Terris Moore made the first ascent of Minya Konka (7,556 m), the highest peak in the Daxue Shan range. Their Sikong Expedition also mapped for the first time a group of lower mountains near Minya Konka, ignored for many years but now seeing attempts and successes.

Grosvenor (6,376 m) (named after Gilbert H. Grosvenor, then President of the National Geographic Society, and called Gonga Konga by the Chinese) was attempted in the spring of 2003 by a British team. They were much harassed by the weather and a group of local people seeking the rare caterpillar fungus, which is said to have medical and aphrodisiac uses. In between fungus hunts, the locals also stole most of the base camp food supply. Two routes were tried and then abandoned in heavy powder snow and spindrift. That fall, the well-known British/New Zealand couple, Julie-Ann Clyma and Roger Payne, had their permit for Chomolhari withdrawn at the last moment and decided to try (quite unofficially) Grosvenor instead. They set up a 4,200-m base camp on October 21, then rested before starting up the NW Face on November 3. They bivouacked on the SW ridge at 5,900 m, moved up the ridge to 6,100 m, slept again, and reached the summit for the first ascent on November 5, 2003. They then climbed down the unexplored E Ridge and rappelled down the icy S Face to reach a col between Grosvenor and the neighboring Jiazi. After another night out, they reached base camp. They met there a group of Chinese Mountaineering Association officials reconnoitering the area for a mountaineering camp; the officials listened sympathetically to the Chomolhari permit story and later helped them legalize their status.

Another supposedly unclimbed peak in the group, named Edgar (6,618 m) after a Western archeologist with the China Inland Mission, was attempted by Britons Angela Bentham, Chris Drinkwater, Titch Kavangh, and Andrew Phillips. At the last moment, they learned of a previously unreported ascent of the S Face by a South Korean group in 2002. They decided to try the more difficult N Face, but on April 20, 2004, found that a serac barrier on the face was too dangerous and retreated.

In another of the endemic permit difficulties, Jo Kippax and Sean Waters of New Zealand were informed on their arrival at Chengdu in September 2004 that their expedition to the eastern Nyanchen Tanglha was canceled. They headed instead for unclimbed **Daddomain** (6,380 m) and **Longemain** (6,294 m) north of Minya Konka. These peaks are on the main ridge between

Minya Konka and Grosvenor and had apparently never been attempted. Approaching from the west, the pair—who had no photographs—reconnoitered the two peaks and decided to try the W Ridge of Longemain from an advanced base camp at 4,700 m. After climbing a long couloir of unconsolidated snow in frequent thunderstorms and establishing a snow cave camp on the ridge, they returned to advanced base. In a three-day push from there, they climbed the rest of the ridge and reached the summit of Longemain to make the first ascent on October 20, 2004. Eyeing Daddomain, Kippax and Waters then decided to attempt the W Ridge of that mountain. Again, a long and dangerous couloir led to the top of the ridge, where they bivouacked in a crevasse. Moving up the steep ridge, they set camp 2 at about 5,800 m. In the cold of late October, they traversed around the western subsidiary peak and reached the summit of Daddomain proper at 4:00 P.M. on October 29, thus completing the first ascents of two almost unexplored, glaciated mountains.

In summer 2002, an American group led by Pete Athans visited the northern Jarjinjabo range in west Szechuan, one of the areas publicized by Nakamura's beautiful photographs. The group made repeat ascents—by new routes—of the dramatic, slender spire called Jammo Spire, first climbed by Japanese the year before, and made two routes on an apparently previously unclimbed prominent broad tower, which they named **Jarjinabo**, though it is not the highest mountain in the range. Between the Szechuan–Tibet border and Namcha Barwa lies the Kangri Garpo range, little explored by mountaineers until recently. There were Japanese reconnaissance expeditions in 1999, 2000, and 2002, and a New Zealand expedition has looked at some of the glaciers. In 2003, a nine-member Kobe University team led by Kazumasa Hirai made an attempt on the highest summit, Ruoni (6,882 m), by the NE Ridge. They reached a col at 5,850 m on October 21, but further progress was prevented by heavy snowfall. No doubt, Hirai will be back. He led the expedition that made the first ascent of Kulu Kangri on the Tibet-Bhutan border in 1986 and has spent much of the time since negotiating permission for Ruoni.

The eastern and western Nyanchen Tanglha ranges lie, respectively, NE and NW of Lhasa. This relative proximity to the capital makes it easier to straighten out permit misunderstandings. In one such incident, Gabriel Voide, a guide from Saas Fee in Switzerland, and two companions finally received permission to attempt **Jieqinnalagabu** (6,316 m) in the eastern range. (The peak is probably the one identified by botanist-explorer Frank Kingdon-Ward in 1924 as Namla Karpo; Kingdon-Ward's names are easier to pronounce.) The group decided to attempt the NW Spur from an advanced base at 4,700 m.

After a week of bad weather and a look at the lower part of the route, Voide's companions bowed out. Starting at 1:00 A.M. Voide made a continuous push to the summit, which he reached in just ten hours. He was forced to down climb the route until he reached rock, after which he combined rappels and down climbing to reach advanced base at 6:00 P.M. A most remarkable solo first ascent of a mountain attempted only twice before.

In the western Nyanchen Tanglha range, the highest summit, Nyanchen Tanglha proper (7,162 m), has been climbed frequently as has the slightly lower Central Summit. But in spring 2002, an Austrian father-son team, Erich and Stefan Gatt, led a commercial group to the top of the Central Summit, then diverted to place a high camp at 6,200 m. From this camp the pair climbed the SW Ridge of the **SE Summit of Nyanchen Tanglha** (7,046 m) to the top, an apparent first ascent.

In far western Tibet, there is an isolated massif north of Gurla Mandata called the Nganglong Kangri Range. In 2004, Americans John Town and Derek Buckle, Martin Scott from the UK, and Toto Gronlund of Finland made the 1,500 km drive from Kathmandu to the area. There are said to be more than 40 peaks over 6,000 m in the massif, but the line of permanent snow is very high in dry western Tibet, and most of the summits are relatively easy to reach — should anyone try. In addition to a good bit of exploration and mapping, the group made two first ascents (or anyway "first ascents by tourists"): **Kang Ngolok I** (6,710 m) and **Kang Ngolok I East** (6,595 m).

Because Bhutan severely limits mountaineering activity, there is a group of unclimbed mountains higher than 7,000 m along the border between Bhutan and China. It is, however, sometimes possible to get permission from the Chinese authorities to attempt these border peaks. Among them is probably the highest unclimbed independent mountain remaining — Gangkar Punzum (7,541 m). This peak has not been opened by the Chinese, but in 2002 a South Korean expedition led by Nam Young-Ho was able to wangle permission to try **Kangphu Gang** (7,204 m) in the adjacent Lunana group. On September 7, 2002, the expedition established a base camp north of the mountain and two more camps on the snow and ice face below the SW Ridge. After reaching a top camp on the ridge, Nam, Li Fua-Fun, Li Ji-Ryue, Chuen Oir, and Kim Ze-Yong continued up the ridge and reached the summit for the first ascent on September 29, 2002.

Julie-Ann Clyma and Roger Payne finally got their **Chomolhari** (7,315 m) permit in spring 2004 and made the first serious attempt on the N side of the mountain. After careful reconnaissance of the N and W faces, they chose a route on the NW Ridge. They spent six days on the route's lower section, then pulled back in very high winds. With little time remaining, they decided to look at the easier S Ridge, climbed by Japanese in 1996. They negotiated a difficult icefall to reach the ridge at 5,800 m and were harassed again by wind for a day, but by midnight on May 6, the winds had dropped, and they set off at 1:30 A.M., May 7, for the summit. They reached it in good weather and returned to the ridge camp by 5:00 P.M. that day. This was the eighth ascent overall, and the first alpine ascent of the route—not necessarily of the mountain. The first ascent of Chomolhari by F. Spencer Chapman and Pasang Dawa Lama in 1936, also ending on the S Ridge, can be described as an alpine ascent.

Shisha Pangma (8,027 m), the only 8,000 meter peak whose summit lies entirely in China, had never been climbed in the winter before 2003. This distinction was caused by Chinese unwillingness to allow winter attempts. Permits were issued for the first time in winter 2003–4. (In common with Nepal, China defines "mountaineering winter" as the period between December 1 and February 15.) The first attempt, by Britons Victor Saunders and Andy Parkin, got no higher than 6,500 m on the SW Face. They were followed by a largely Polish group incorporating the well-known Italian Himalayan climber Simone Moro. The Poles long record of first winter ascents of 8,000ers is based on the calendar definition of winter as starting on December 21. Moro and Piotr Morawski reached the top of the SW Face in January, certainly deep winter by anyone's definition. Faced with -50° C cold, they were unable to continue to the summit and had to be content with the first winter ascent of the SW Face. The more legalistically minded Jean Christophe Lafaille came to the mountain in November 2004 with a plan for a solo ascent of the mountain by the SW Face in the warmer days of early December. He fixed some rope and returned to his base camp, then started up again on November 26, pushed the route further to a camp at 7,100 m, and climbed down to wait for better weather. On December 7, the weather improved, and he returned to the 7,100 m camp. Leaving that camp, he climbed to the summit and returned during the night of December 10–11. He had managed the first winter ascent under the Chinese rules, a solo at that—no one else even on the mountain—and he was granted a certificate to prove it. But not so fast—Moro and the Poles returned in late December 2004, this time to try the Slovenian Route. On January 13, 2005, Moro and Morawski reached the top, certainly well into calendar winter. They also appear to have obtained a "first winter ascent" certificate from the Chinese. If Moro's claim is accepted, he will be the first (and only) non-Pole to make the first winter ascent of an 8,000er—albeit as a member of a Polish expedition.

Nepal Himalaya

The Maoist insurgency and general political unrest in Nepal continue, indeed may have worsened. Maoist-forced contributions from mountaineers and trekkers in the backcountry, strikes, extortion from backcountry hotels and lodges, and the occasional bus burning or explosion proceed unabated. King Gyanendra governs by fiat, and most formal political processes are in abeyance. The situation has attained the dignity of a *New York Times* Travel article, reporting a 30-percent decrease in tourism. Certainly Kathmandu has seen a loss in sales in the Thamel shops and low occupancy in the hotels and guest houses.

The effect of all this on mountaineering is not so obvious. Most mountaineering trips to the Himalaya involve long-term planning and advance financial commitment, and it is not easy to divert to a new objective in a different country. Mountaineers in Nepal have grown accustomed to the periodic shakedowns by supposed Maoists and view them as merely another cost of mountaineering in the country. So far, there appear to be few examples of serious violence directed at mountaineers or tourists.

In fact, activity on **Everest** (8,848 m) has actually increased in the past two seasons. In 2002, when the insurgency and governmental difficulties were already apparent, there were 159 ascents of the mountain, a drop in number from the previous year. In 2003, with unrest more critical, there were 267 ascents—an all time record. This increase was said to be the result of the celebration on the mountain in honor of the 50th anniversary of the first ascent. But then in 2004, with the situation still more critical and no anniversary celebration, there were 331 ascents.

Clearly, the most important of these ascents in pre-monsoon 2004 was the first recognized new route on Everest in eight years, created by a Russian team on the N Face. The effort was a typically Russian, heavy project, with a team of fifteen climbers and three climbing Sherpas transporting 2,500 kg of food and 5,000 m of rope up the face. The team set up a base camp at 6,200 m at the foot of the face on April 6, and made careful preparations. Then, in the usual Russian deliberate style, four rotating teams of strong climbers ground out a fully fixed route more or less directly up the steep slope toward the summit. The steady progress was marked by the establishment of camp 1 at 7,100 m on April 20, camp 2 at 7,550 m on April 28, camp 3 at 7,850 m on May 11 and, finally, camp 4 at 8,300 m. On May 27, Andrey Mariev, Pavel Shabalin, and Iliyas Tukhvatullin climbed to camp 4 and set out the following morning for the summit. They reached 8,600 m that evening and slept in a makeshift camp 5. On May 29, the leader, Shabalin, found that progress directly upward on the Yellow Band was far too slow. The three retreated to camp 5, considered the matter, and decided to divert from the direct path to the summit. The following morning they traversed left to the edge of the Great Couloir and, bypassing the steepest rock above the Yellow Band, reached the summit at 10:00 A.M. on May 30. The route was repeated by other team members on May 31 and June 1.

The new route, already dubbed "The Russian Direct," is not quite that. The diversion through the Yellow Band to the Great Couloir and the bypass-ing of the great rock cliff are the sorts of things that someone will feel obliged to rectify some day. Nevertheless, the route is a remarkable monument to the Russian team's efficiency and dogged persistence.

In sharp contrast to the long Russian effort, a Sherpa named Pemba Dorje claimed he had made the trip from the Khumbu base camp on the S side to the summit in 8 hours and 8 minutes during the night of May 20–1, 2004. He said he used oxygen only above 7,900 m. This climb was his second speed ascent — in 2003 he reached the summit on the same route in 12 hours and 45 minutes — but his record held only three days, until Lhakpa Gelu cut the time to 10 hours and 56 minutes. No one seems to have witnessed Pemba Dorje's 2004 climb; indeed, no one else summited on May 21 from either side. There was a degree of incredulity about the major improvement between his two speed climbs, a reduction in time to the top of 38 percent, but the Ministry of Tourism officially ratified the ascent, leaving the question, How do they know? (Apparently in response to this question, in 2005 the Ministry inau-gurated a "working procedure" for ratifying mountaineering feats. They will require unambiguous summit photographs, preferably dated and timed, cop-ies of any photographs taken with other climbers, and a full written report.)

There was little remarkable about all the other ascents, and there were few new "minor distinctions." Among the latter, Lhakpa Sherpa became the first woman to make four ascents of Everest. But climbing Everest is never routine. Seven died on the mountain, the worst record since 1997. On the N Side, Shoko Ota, who, at 63, had just become the second-oldest woman to climb Everest, collapsed and died on her way down. A well-known Bulgarian climber named Hristo Hristov also died on the way down after his summit climb without supplemental oxygen, and another Bulgarian, Mariana Maslaova, died on the way up. Two Koreans, Jang Min and Park Mu-Taek died on the descent after reaching the top, and expedition leader, Baek Joon-Ho, died of exhaustion in his attempt to rescue them. On the S Side, 68-year-old American Nils Antzana died on the way down the S Col Route after reaching the summit.

Of course, the outstanding news from the 2004 pre-monsoon season was the Russian first direct climb of the N Face of **Jannu** (7,710 m), covered at length in "Alpina" for Summer/Fall 2005. As expected, the jury of mountaineering establishment stalwarts at the February 2005 Piolet d'Or award meeting in Grenoble voted to give the award for the "most outstanding achievement in the world of Alpinism during 2004" to the obviously difficult ascent, though it was achieved in an outdated "heavy style." There was a divided vote and considerable criticism from the audience. The organizers of the ceremony, *Montagnes* magazine and the Groupe de Haute Montagne of the French Alpine Club, initiated a "People's Prize" to be awarded by the vote of the 850 spectators, who chose the solo climb of K7 in Pakistan by American Steve House.

Eight expeditions tried **Makalu** (8,463 m); the four on the Standard NW Ridge Route put a total of fourteen climbers on the summit. More interesting were the other four expeditions attempting new routes or routes not used for years. The most impressive of these was a solo exploit by Jean Christophe Lafaille, who planned to climb **Makalu II** (7,678 m) from Tibet, then descend to the Makalu La and follow the NW Ridge to the top of Makalu for his twelfth 8,000er ascent. From a base camp on the Kangchung Glacier, Lafaille established an advanced base camp—all alone—below the N Face of Makalu II at 5,750 m. Lafaille reached the NW Ridge relatively easily, but found progress along the ridge the hardest thing he had done at such an altitude. He made several climbs up and down for acclimatization, then descended to his base camp for a good rest. On May 13, he set out for his final attempt, attained his previous high point on the afternoon of May 14, and reached 7,400 m and slept there on May 15. At 2:00 P.M. May 16, he reached the top of Makalu II and descended a short distance to bivouac for the night. The next day he descended easily to the Makalu La and slept again. However, the next morning he found he was too exhausted to face the climb to Makalu summit and descended into Nepal. There it became obvious that his presence was not authorized, and he scampered back into Tibet, reaching his base camp seven days after leaving it. Lafaille failed to tick off another 8,000er but is credited with the first ascent of Makalu II from Tibet.

A British Services expedition attempted a repeat of Makalu SE Ridge, which has not been climbed since 1995. They were joined partway up by members of a French expedition. The British gave up on May 24 due to heavy snowfall and unstable conditions. The French (Yannick Graziani, Christian Trommsdorff, and Patrick Wagnon) had descended to their Tibetan base camp for a rest and returned to the abandoned British camp 2 on May 26. The next day they reached 7,300 m, where they dug out a British tent, and on May 28 they reached 7,600 m. That night, the wind was estimated at nearly 100 km/hr and the trio, having only an inner tent and two sleeping bags to cover all three, suffered severely. The wind dropped the next morning but the slope was steep, and first Trommsdorf, then Wagnon turned back. Graziani made the top at 4:30 P.M., probably the first time anyone has climbed directly from the lower SE Ridge all the way to the summit. He made his way down to his two companions by 8:00 P.M., and all reached base camp on May 31.

Maxut Zhumayev's Kazakh Expedition put four members on the summit via the W Pillar Route, which had not been climbed since 1991, but the first summit pair, Vladislav Terzyul and Jay Sieger (an American) fell on the descent. Sieger's body was found by Vassily Pivtsov and Zhumayev (who both later summited), but Terzyul was never found. He was a distinguished Himalyan climber and a Snow Leopard (one who has climbed all the 7,000 m peaks in the former Soviet Union). Counting his Makalu summit, Terzyul had climbed thirteen of the fourteen 8,000ers and the Central Summit of Shisha Pangma, all without supplementary oxygen.

Pakistan and the Karakoram

As in Nepal, internal unrest and threats of terrorism have had an adverse effect on tourism and probably on mountaineering in Pakistan. The government has reacted by relaxing regulations, particularly for mountains less than 6,500 m, and by cutting all peak fees in half. The fee reduction has been extended for the 2005 season, and there is talk of abolishing all peak fees for mountains below 7,000 m. The result is that recorded activity is mostly by commercial groups and is largely confined to the 8,000 m peaks and the popular Diran and Spantik.

Much of this activity is on the easiest routes and has little intrinsic interest. However on **K2** (8,611 m), the 2004 season saw the first successful ascents since 2001. The reasons for the hiatus were fears of terrorism, bad weather, and a collapse of the serac forming one side of the "Bottleneck" feature at 8,300 m on the Normal Abruzzi Ridge Route, making that route more difficult. The damage seemed less troublesome in 2004, and the season was the 50th anniversary of the first ascent of K2 by Italians Achille Compagnoni and Lino Lacedelli in 1954, so when the weather improved toward the end of July, many climbers were in place, ready to try the ascent. By the end of July, 47 had made the top. Among these were two "legacy" ascents, by Michele Compagnoni (grandson of Achille) and Mario Lacedelli (nephew of Lino). Basques Edurne Pasaban and Juanito Oiarzabal reached the top late on July 26, the seventh 8,000er for Pasaban. Of course, Oiarzabal, who finished the 8,000er list in 1999, had been up K2 before—indeed, he has reached the top of an 8,000 m peak 21 times. Pasaban returned to a camp on the Shoulder that evening, but Oiarzabal only reached a point about 100 m above the tent and sat out all night. Both suffered frostbitten feet; Pasaban lost two toes, and Oiarzabal is far more seriously damaged.

The most remarkable performance on the mountain was the second ascent of the SSW Ridge, the "Magic Line"—so named by Reinhold Messner but never actually tried by him. The route, very direct and technically very difficult, has a short and tragic climbing history. In 1986, Renato Casarotto made repeated attempts at a solo ascent and died in a crevasse on the relatively flat glacier below. In that same tragic season, Slovak Peter Bozik, and Poles Przemyslaw Piasecki and Wojciech Wroz completed the route, but Wroz fell to his death on his way down the Abruzzi Ridge. The 2004 climb was a three-month project by the Spanish group, Oscar Cadiach, Jordi Corominas, Manuel de la Matta, Jordi Tosas, and Valen Giro. They established four camps up the Magic Line, the highest at 8,100 m. On August 16, Cadiach, de La Matta, and Corominas started for the summit. Corominas was moving better than Cadiach and de La Matta, and the latter two decided to turn back at 8,300 m. Corominas had trouble with deep snow and finally reached the summit at midnight, the 48th ascent for the season. He then descended to reach camp 3 after 30 hours on the go. Cadiach and de La Matta also descended without much problem, but at camp 1 on August 18, de La Matta suddenly complained of abdominal pain and breathing difficulty and died the following morning.

Deadly K2 exacted other penalties for the 48 ascents. Around June 11,

K2 from the south showing the "Magic Line." First ascent of this line by the Polish/ Slovak expedition in 1986. Second ascent by Jordi Corominas in 2004. (The trace of the Magic Line is superimposed on Vittorio Sella's magnificent 1909 photograph, which is reproduced from a print in the AMC Sella Collection.)

three Koreans on a "cleanup" expedition were buried in their tent at camp 1 by an avalanche, and all died. In late July, Davoud Asl of Iran, Sergei Sokolov of Russia, and Kazakh Alexander Gubaev were encamped high on the mountain. Gubaev left for a summit try on July 28; his companions decided to wait for better weather. Gubaev is thought to have reached the summit but never returned. Asl and Sokolov, perhaps already hypoxic, could not be persuaded to descend and were trapped by a storm. They started down on August 1, but there was no further word. Climbers at base camp started a rescue effort but had to abandon it in heavy snowfall.

Gasherbrum III (7,953 m) is commonly listed as the fifteenth highest independent mountain in the world, ranking just after the usual list of the fourteen 8,000ers. Because it does not reach the magic 8,000 m line, it has been relatively neglected — before 2004, there had been only one ascent, by a Polish expedition in 1975. (The summit team for the first ascent incorporated Allison Chadwick and Wanda Rutkiewicz; thus Gasherbrum III is the highest mountain to have had a female contingent in the first ascent party.) The 2004 attempt was by Basques Jon Beloki, Alberto Iñurrategi, and José Carlos Tamayo. They placed camps up the original route and set off from camp 4 on July 29, Tamayo turned back, but the others reached the summit for the second ascent. Iñurrategi completed the fourteen 8,000ers in 2002, so he is the only man to have climbed the fifteen highest mountains in the world.

Steve House led an expedition of Americans and the Slovenian Marko Prezelj to the Charakusa valley in June 2004. Although the valley is next to the extensively mountaineered Baltoro, the group found opportunities for a wealth of new routes and first ascents. On July 24 and 25, House made a new solo route on **K7** (6,934 m) via the SW Face. This was only the second climb of K7 since the 1983 first ascent by a Japanese team. Later Doug Chabot and Bruce Miller repeated the Japanese Route in alpine style and descended by the new House Route. As covered elsewhere in these notes, the House solo won the "People's Choice" award at the February 2005 Piolet d'Or ceremonies in Grenoble.

Climbing All Fourteen 8,000-Meter Peaks

In "Alpina" for Winter/Spring 2005, I pointed out that at least three Western climbers, American Ed Viesturs, South Tyrolean (Italian) Christian Kuntner, and Briton Alan Hinkes, were poised to join the exclusive and dangerous peak-bagging club founded by Reinhold Messner in 1986. The fate of all three is now known. Viesturs was the first to finish all fourteen 8,000ers, reaching the summit of Annapurna via the original N Side French Route on May 12, 2005, to become the twelfth member of the club and the first from the United States. (Carlos Carsolio of Mexico completed his fourteen in 1996, and thus, I suppose, ranks as the senior "American" member.)

Christian Kuntner also needed Annapurna and was climbing the French Route with Aosta guide Abele Blanc (who had also accumulated thirteen 8,000ers) when both were struck by a serac fall on May 18, 2005. Blanc survived; Kuntner died. He is the second man, after Benoit Chamoux on Kanchenjunga in 1995, to die on the way up the last peak required for membership.

Alan Hinkes, who lacked Kanchenjunga to complete the set, reached the top of that mountain on May 30, 2005 in a driving snowstorm and claimed membership — supported by the trumpeting of his commercial sponsors. Unfortunately, a controversy surfaced over his 1990 ascent of 8,201 m Cho Oyo. That year, Hinkes was a member of an international group of climbers nominally led by Benoit Chamoux. Chamoux reported that seven members, including himself and Hinkes, reached the summit on April 30, 1990. After Chamoux's death, at least one of the seven reported that none had reached the summit and that all had retreated in heavy mist from about 8,100 m. So far, those who keep the count have not accepted Hinkes's claim to all fourteen. Cho Oyo is the easiest of the 8,000ers, but Hinkes has shown little inclination to repeat the climb for the benefit of the doubters.

Basque Edurne Pasaban is the leading female candidate for membership. With her climb of K2 in July 2004, she has accumulated seven of the fourteen, more than any other woman except the late Wanda Rutkiewicz. Pasaban has climbed five of the six highest mountains in the world, and also holds an ominous distinction: the only woman who has reached the summit of K2 and is still alive.

In Memoriam

Andreas (Anderl) Heckmair, 1906–2005. In 1938, German climbers Anderl Heckmair and Ludwig Vörg met Austrians Heinrich Harrer and Fritz Kasparek on the lower part of the already infamous North Face of the Eiger. They knew each other by reputation as members of the school of German, Austrian, and Italian climbers — considered extreme — who were willing to attempt the difficult and certainly dangerous Alpine faces that had previously been considered out of bounds for "true mountaineers." The Eiger North Face had become the symbol for all that the true mountaineers criticized. Eight men had died in unsuccessful attempts and, since all these attempts had been made by climbers from Nazi and Fascist countries, there were accusations of dark Teutonic or Fascist death wishes on the part of the climbers and of government subsidies or bribes to gain propaganda benefits in the ideological struggles leading up to the start of World War II.

To avoid the attention of Swiss authorities, who tried to discourage climbing on the wall, the four had made furtive and inconspicuous approaches, but they were now clearly seen from the hotel telescopes at Kleine Scheidegg. It would be dangerous and inefficient for the two parties to proceed independently, so they joined forces. Heckmair and Vörg were more experienced and better equipped, and Heckmair was chosen to lead the joint party up the wall. In 61 hours, the Eiger North Face was climbed despite a severe storm.

Regardless of the degree of Nazi party involvement before the climb, the Nazis seized on the publicity bonanza associated with the success. There was a visit with Hitler, decorations, a Scandinavian cruise, and sinecures for all at the SS *Ordensburg* training school at Sonthofen. Unlike Harrer, Heckmair apparently never actually joined the SS, nor did he adjust well to Nazi discipline. After the start of the Russian campaign, he was sent to the eastern front—not a mark of Nazi favor. He survived for six months and was then rescued by the intervention of an officer friend at the army mountaineering training school near Innsbruck. Heckmair spent the rest of the war as a climbing instructor, and at war's end in 1945, he simply walked away over the mountains to Oberstdorf and set himself up as a guide.

He had a long and successful career as a mountaineering instructor and guide, traveling widely in the world's mountains and continuing to act as a guide until his late 80s. While he did not have the sort of literary success attained by Harrer with *Seven Years in Tibet*, *The White Spider*, and other works, Heckmair's 1972 mountaineering autobiography (English title: *My Life as a Mountaineer*) was a good tale and sold well.

Perhaps the best comment on the prewar mountaineering establishment's belief that those who attempted the Eiger North Face were subject to dark Teutonic, Fascist, or Nietzschean death wishes is to note that of the four who made the first ascent of the Eiger North Face, only one, Fritz Kasparek, died in the mountains. Kasparek fell through a cornice on Salcantay while climbing in South America after the war. Ludwig Vörg died on the Russian front the first day of the campaign, as millions of German and Russian soldiers were to do later. Heckmair, after a long and adventurous mountaineering career died, apparently in bed, at 98. Harrer, now 93, is still alive and still writing.

Acknowledgments. These notes are based in part on accounts published in High Mountain Magazine, Climb Magazine, *and the* American Alpine Journal. *The use of the valuable reference source,* The Himalayan Database, *is also gratefully acknowledged.*

—*Jeffery Parrette*
"Alpina" Editor

Interlude

On the cusp of the first day of spring a late snowstorm
      Staggers in dragging its frustrations along the mountain
To plop down for several hours like an ale-addled uncle
    Unveiling muffled tales of distant towns before heading south
For the coast glossing over each green nubbin of growth
    Which sprouted outside this window along the porch rail
Or past the cedar run where it slopes suddenly to scree
    Each impatient sprig of life which seems oblivious to such
Stupor roiling overhead like a head overrun with bad ideas
    But while the temperatures slowly rise the squalls continue
Unevenly tensile as if fading in and out of consciousness
    Until there's only muddle amid the slurs of slate gray sky
And a thick floc of pine boughs bowing ever so sheepishly
    Across the path so the moment comes when attention stops
And silence begins again waiting here like a pressed flower
    Or a truth and after the silence a killdeer hovering above
The clearing lands finally in protest and the hermit thrush
    Thrusts upward as if carrying song into the air is enough

—*Larry Bradley*

LARRY BRADLEY's work has appeared in *The Paris Review, Poetry Northwest,* and *Western Humanities Review.* He currently lives and writes in Vermont's Northeast Kingdom.

News and Notes

Renovation of Cardigan Lodge Completed. The AMC's Cardigan Lodge re-opened for guests last summer, with a $1.5 million renovation completed. Extensive remodeling of the two upper floors increased the lodge's capacity to sixty guests in thirteen bunkrooms and two private rooms. The bunkrooms feature new bedding and furniture (locally made from sustainably harvested wood), including rock maple-framed beds. Other interior improvements include a mudroom and library on the first floor, a modernized and expanded restroom on the second floor, and energy-efficient windows. The building also sports a new steel roof and several dormers. The grounds around the lodge were tilled and seeded to combat a wetness problem that had been leading to erosion.

The AMC's High Cabin, located high on the slope of Cardigan's South Peak, was also recently renovated. This rustic retreat was built in 1931 by William F. Gillman. In 2004 it was equipped with new bunk beds, roof, woodstove and Clivus composting toilet, and its capacity was expanded to twelve people.

Source: The Record Enterprise, Plymouth, NH (Stephen Garfield); AMC website (www.outdoors.org)

Trail Bridges Washed Out by Spring Floods. Unusually heavy spring rains combined with snowmelt and ice jams to destroy or cause major damage to a number of trail bridges in the White Mountains. According to the U.S. Forest Service and the Randolph Mountain Club, it is anticipated that most or all of these bridges will be replaced, though the timetable is uncertain. In the meantime, hikers were advised to use caution on these trails, especially during periods of high water. Among the bridges affected:

- The 26-foot bridge over the North Branch of the Gale River on the Gale River Trail, 1.7 miles from the trailhead. This crossing can be made on rocks but could be difficult at times.
- Spider Bridge over the Wild River at the 2.7-mile mark on the Wild River Trail. Two of the four spans on this 86-foot bridge were washed away, and the remaining spans were unstable. This would be a very difficult crossing without a bridge.

- The 42-foot bridge over the Zealand River on the Trestle Trail near Sugarloaf Campground, another very difficult crossing.
- The 100-foot suspension bridge over the Dry River at the 1.7-mile mark on the Dry River Trail. The main cable suspension brackets were pulled out of the deck beams and the bridge was immediately closed for safety reasons. Without the bridge this is a very difficult crossing at high water in a valley that drains very rapidly.
- The 26-foot Carolyn Cutter Stevens Memorial Bridge over Snyder Brook on the Randolph Path and Brookside, 0.9 mile from the Appalachia trailhead. At normal water levels this crossing can usually be made on rocks.
- Baldwin Bridge over the Moose River on the Bee Line in Randolph. This bridge was soon repaired.
- The 40-foot bridge over Clay Brook on the Jewell Trail, 1.1 mile from the trailhead. At normal water levels this crossing can be made on rocks.
- The 40-foot bridge over Morrison Brook on the west end of the Caribou Trail in Evans Notch, 0.4 mile from the trailhead. Wading may be required at all but the lowest water levels.
- A 30-foot bridge over Rob Brook on the Rob Brook Trail was heavily damaged, caution should be used.
- A 30-foot bridge over the Cutler River on the Huntington Ravine winter access route was damaged but was soon repaired.

Sources: White Mountain National Forest website (www.fs.fed.us/r9/white); Randolph Mountain Club

Hayden Grant Extends Reach of YOP Program. The AMC has received a $150,000 grant from the Charles Hayden Foundation to support its Youth Opportunities Program (YOP), which is dedicated to making the outdoors and the environment accessible and meaningful to youth. This grant builds on the success of the AMC's partnership with the Charles Hayden Foundation last summer and allows the AMC to reach a larger number of urban youth in Boston neighborhoods throughout the year. The AMC will partner directly with five Boston youth agencies focused on providing services to at-risk youth. The five agencies are Catholic Charities' St. Peter's Teen Center, Dorchester Youth Collaborative, Inquilinos Boricuas En Acción (IBA), Salvation Army Boston South End Corps and Boston Central Branch YMCA. The grant will allows the program to serve 500 young people from summer 2005 through spring 2006, in addition to 3,500 youth that the program already benefits each year. The program also will train as many as 10 agency staff at the five organizations and provide guidance, support, and mentoring.

Source: AMC website (www.outdoors.org/education)

Reconstruction of Bunnell Notch Trail Highlights Recreation Fee Projects.
One of the most significant projects funded in 2004 by the White Mountain National Forest (WMNF) Parking Pass Program was a major reconstruction of the Bunnell Notch Trail in the Kilkenny region. This eastern approach to Mount Cabot, the northernmost of the New Hampshire 4000-footers, has seen a significant increase in usage since the closure of the shorter western approach by a private landowner in 2000. The trail had become notably muddy and eroded in places. The trail crew relocated about 0.5 mile of the trail and installed 126 step stones, 6 rock staircases with cribbing, 12 rock water bars, 20 drainage dips, 6 bog bridges, 27 check dams and staggered steps, 115 feet of log rock box, and 270 feet of side and cross drainages.

The USFS also worked with the Wonalancet Out Door Club to rehabilitate the severely eroded Lawrence Trail on Mount Paugus, building twenty rock steps, six rock waterbars, and four rock check dams.

Other projects completed on the WMNF included rehabilitation of a bridge on the Huntington Ravine Fire Road; improvements at the trailhead for the Piper Trail to Mount Chocorua; a 1.3 mile relocation at the south end of the Moat Mountain Trail, including construction of a 40-foot steel stringer bridge over Dry Brook, plus a new trailhead parking area; the reconstruction of several existing trailhead information kiosks; and the installation of several new kiosks, including an interpretive display for the Sandwich Range Wilderness at the Ferncroft trailhead in Wonalancet and another at Lincoln Woods on the Kancamagus Highway. The USFS also purchased supplies and materials to support the AMC/Forest Service Alpine Steward volunteers, who help educate hikers about alpine zone ecology on popular Franconia Ridge.

In 2004 a total of $570,469 was collected in Parking Pass fees, a slight decrease from 2003. The seven-year total from 1998–2004 was $4,476,550.

The initial "Fee Demo" program, begun in 1996, was set to expire at the end of 2005. In December 2004, President Bush signed into law the Federal Lands Recreation Enhancement Act (FLREA). The enactment of FLREA extends the recreation fee program for 10 years, with some modifications to address public concerns about the program. It applies to recreation lands managed by the U.S. Forest Service, Bureau of Land Management, and other Federal agencies.

Under the new law fees are limited to sites that have a specified minimum level of development and that meet specific criteria. There are also requirements to provide the public with information on fees and on how fee revenues will be used.

In response to the standards set under the new law, the Forest Service announced in 2005 that fees would no longer be required at 500 picnic areas and trailheads across the country, including ten on the WMNF. For a site to require a fee, it must have designated parking, an interpretive or educational component, a toilet, picnic facilities, garbage collection, and/or routine security.

On the WMNF, the fee boxes were slated to be removed from the Tunnel Brook Trail, Town Line Trail, and Blueberry Mountain Trail trailheads near Glencliff; the Beaver Brook Trail trailhead in Kinsman Notch in Woodstock; the Ravine Lodge Road trailhead for Mount Moosilauke on Route 118; Breezy Point in Warren, at the base of Mount Moosilauke; the Hancock scenic overlook on the Kancamagus Highway, which is also the trailhead for the Hancock Notch Trail; the trailhead for Mountain Pond Loop Trail on Slippery Brook Road between Jackson and North Conway; and the parking areas for Elbow Pond and Beaver Pond in Woodstock.

Source: WMNF Recreation Fee 2004 Annual Report; *The Union Leader*, Manchester, NH (Paula Tracy)

Vyron D. Lowe Trail Relocated. The Randolph Mountain Club (RMC) completed a major relocation of the Vyron D. Lowe Trail in the summer of 2005. The new path, 1.6 miles long, provides a route from Randolph Spring on Durand Road in Randolph to the Crescent Ridge Trail just west of the fine viewpoint at Lookout Ledge.

Vyron D. Lowe was long a prominent citizen in Randolph and was a mountain guide, a game warden, a chewing-gum manufacturer, and the proprietor of Lowe's Store. Upon his death in 1961, an existing trail leading from Lowe's to the Pond of Safety was named the Vyron D. Lowe Trail in his memory. In 1981, this trail was closed by lumbering, and the RMC cut a new trail to Lookout Ledge and named it, in turn, the Vyron D. Lowe Trail. This route, however, was muddy and erosion-prone, so in the summers of 2004 and 2005, the RMC trail crew and volunteers relocated the trail again. The new path is less steep and uses more switchbacks to traverse the steeper terrain. Lookout Ledge is noted for its exceptional view of the Northern Presidentials and King Ravine.

Source: Randolph Mountain Club

RMC Publishes Revamped Guidebook. Last summer, the Randolph Mountain Club published an expanded and completely revised new edition of its venerable guidebook, *Randolph Paths: Guide to the Northern Presidentials and the Crescent Range*. This is the eighth edition of the guide, which was first published in 1917, ten years after the initial publication of what is today the AMC White Mountain Guide. The revised RMC guide includes all new trail descriptions compiled by a team of a dozen volunteers. Newly described are the recently built trails in the Randolph Community Forest and the trails at the nearby Pondicherry National Wildlife Refuge. An expanded section on suggested walks includes route summaries to the Northern Peaks and recommended ski and snowshoe trips.

An expanded RMC trails history, written by club historian Judy Hudson, includes a number of newly uncovered historical photographs, as well as interesting discoveries. One of these is the story of what is perhaps the oldest trail sign in existence for the region, for Cascade Ravine's Pioneer Spring. The new guide also offers extensive information on snowshoeing and backcountry skiing; geology highlights by Bates College professor Dyk Eusden; a new section devoted to the flora of the mountains by Brad Meiklejohn; an expanded introduction with Leave No Trace guidelines and information on mountain safety and search and rescue; an expanded Points of Interest section with additional historical information; and a thorough index prepared by archivist Al Hudson.

An updated Tyvek RMC trail map, *Map of Randolph Valley and the Northern Peaks of the Mount Washington Range*, produced by cartographer Jon Hall, was also issued with the guide.

Source: Randolph Mountain Club (www.randolphmountainclub.org)

New Hampshire Conservation Officers Receive Awards. Two New Hampshire Fish and Game Department Conservation Officers, who have been extensively involved in search and rescue operations, have been recognized with awards for outstanding performance.

Lt. Jonas Todd Bogardus, well known and highly respected in the New Hampshire search and rescue community, was honored with the 2004 Shikar-Safari Wildlife Officer of the Year award. Conservation Officer Mark T. Hensel was the recipient of the 2004 Northeast Conservation Law Enforcement Chiefs Association "Officer of the Year" award.

Source: New Hampshire Fish and Game Department

Work Completed by AMC Trail Crews in 2005

AMC's professional and volunteer trail crews had a busy summer. Here are a few highlights from 2005 projects:

Maine Woods Initiative: A new 1.5-mile trail running parallel to Trout Brook will provide ski (and hiking) access to Long Pond from the Hedgehog checkpoint area. A side trail along the way takes you to Trout Pond, an attractive pond for fly-fishing and moose watching. The trail can be used to access Moose Point Cabin on skis or snowshoes when Long Pond is frozen over. Final touches on the new Laurie's Ledge Trail included a direct trailhead access from Little Lyford Pond Camps and a connection to the Lollipop Loop hiking trail, which will now become a permanent part of the Laurie's Ledge Trail. AMC also graded and removed large obstacles from extensive portions of the Indian Mountain Circuit Trail and the Hedgehog Gate Trail, which will make these trails skiable for longer periods during the winter.

AMC Trail Crew completes work on Cascade Brook bridge at the junction of the Basin-Cascades Trail and the Cascade Brook Trail (AT).

PHOTO COURTESY OF THE AMC PHOTO LIBRARY

Grafton Loop Trail: This fall, AMC completed the final 3.5 miles of the Grafton Loop Trail in the Mahoosucs. The loop trail is approximately 37 miles in total length, and includes approximately 8 miles of the Appalachian Trail. The newly constructed trail on the west side, the portion that AMC will maintain into the future, is about 14 miles long. One designated campsite has been constructed and more will be completed over the coming years. Signs and blazing will be complete in late fall of 2005, making the trail ready for hikers in spring of 2006. Information about the complete loop will soon be available on www.outdoors.org (the current information only covers the eastern portion).

White Mountain National Forest: The AMC Professional Trail Crews installed a 50-foot Fiberglass composite bridge over Cascade Brook at the junction of the Basin-Cascades Trail and the Cascade Brook Trail (AT). The new bridge replaces the bridge that collapsed in 1986. Other summer projects included erosion control work on the Lion's Head Winter Route, re-construction of the north-fork of the Hancock Loop Trail, extensive reconstruction on the lower half of the Fishin' Jimmy Trail, and extensive bog bridge construction on the Ethan Pond Trail. This fall, a White Mountains trail crew of 7 will be doing rock work repair on the Boott Spur Trail, repairing trail at the Blue Hills Reservation outside of Boston, making sections of the Pemi Trail in Franconia Notch skiable, removing an unsafe bridge on the Connie's Way ski trail, brushing out the Kinsman Ridge Trail, and putting the finishing touches on the Grafton Loop Trail.

Berkshires: We had our most successful year to date of the Berkshires Volunteer Trail Crews, with full teen crews throughout the summer repairing sections of the Appalachian Trail in Massachusetts. AMC's Ridgerunners also monitored and maintained the AT in Connecticut, and shared ethical backcountry recreation tips with over 4,000 hikers. In fall of 2005, a trail crew of four will also be spending a couple of weeks addressing trail maintenance on Mt. Greylock.

Volunteer Crews and Training: By the end of October, AMC will have led 56 volunteer trail crews and skills trainings at locations in the White Mountains, at the Grafton Loop Trail, in Acadia National Park, at Baxter State Park, in the Berkshires, at Mount Cardigan, in the Delaware Water Gap, and at the Maine Kathadin Ironworks property. This is in addition to the hundreds of trail work trips led through AMC Chapters and individual AMC volunteer trail adopters.

Source: AMC website (www.outdoors.org/trails)

Land Conservation News

Maine Woods Initiative Receives Major Forest Legacy Grant. In August 2005, the AMC and The Trust for Public Land announced Congressional approval of $4.5 million in USDA Forest Legacy funding for the Katahdin Iron Works (KIW) Project in central Maine, a cornerstone of AMC's Maine Woods Initiative. The grant was the single largest nationwide out of 40 funded projects. The project has received strong support from U.S. Senators Olympia Snowe and Susan Collins and U.S. Representative Michael Michaud. Governor John Baldacci and the Maine Department of Conservation recommended the KIW project as Maine's top Forest Legacy priority for the year, and the U.S. Forest Service ranked it #4 nationally in the President's FY06 Forest Legacy budget.

The Forest Legacy Program, authorized by Congress in 1990 to keep intact natural and recreational resources of the nation's dwindling forests, provides federal money to states to protect threatened working forests and woodlands either through public purchase or conservation easements. The latter are voluntary agreements in which landowners are paid to give up future development rights on their property. With its minimum requirement of 25 percent non-federal matching funds, the program leverages state and private dollars to complement federal money, creating partnerships that have lasting value.

Source: AMC MWI website (www.outdoors.org/mwi)

Tumbledown Mountain Protected. In the fall of 2004 Maine's Congressional delegation and Governor John E. Baldacci announced the permanent protection of 6,702 acres around Tumbledown Mountain, a spectacular 3090-foot peak in the Weld region. Land formerly owned by MeadWestvaco was purchased by the State of Maine. The deal was negotiated by the Maine Department of Conservation, the Trust for Public Land, and the Tumbledown Conservation Alliance (of which AMC is a member). It is part of a larger effort that has so far protected more than 26,000 acres in the Tumbledown area.

A local, state, federal, and private partnership raised the $2.4 million needed to purchase the land, including $1.5 million from the federal Forest Legacy program and $960,000 from the Land for Maine's Future Program. The land includes trails leading to the summit of Tumbledown, a popular hiking destination known for its great south cliff and picturesque Tumbledown Pond. (Trails in this area are described and mapped in the new *AMC Maine Mountain Guide, 9th edition*.) Sam Hodder of the Trust for Public Land noted that the newly acquired land provides an important link between previously conserved lands. One can now walk on publicly accessible, conserved land for 11 miles from Mount Blue in Mount Blue State Park to Tumbledown Mountain.

Source: Northern Sky News

Lands Protected on Mount Abraham and Saddleback Mountain. In October 2004 the Maine Appalachian Trail Land Trust (MATLT) made its first land acquisitions by purchasing 1,159 acres on the summit and ridgeline of 4050-foot Mount Abraham and 1,183 acres on the southeast slopes of 4120-foot Saddleback Mountain. These two peaks are in the cluster of 4000-footers in the Rangeley–Stratton area. The Appalachian Trail runs along the open ridgeline of Saddleback, and the bare summit of Abraham is accessed from the AT via a side trail. The parcels include parts of the last two remaining high-elevation Maine peaks not protected as public lands or in private conservation transactions.

In 2002 the Appalachian Trail Conference (ATC) transferred 4,033 acres of land it had acquired on Mount Abraham to the State of Maine for the creation of an ecological reserve. However, the mountain's summit and ridgeline remained unprotected. In 2004 the MATLT obtained loans and funding to purchase the remaining areas on the mountain. This land was then transferred to the state and added to the existing reserve. In addition to the extensive alpine habitat on Mount Abraham — in Maine, only Katahdin has a larger area above treeline — the parcel includes old-growth forest at lower elevations.

The MATLT was created in 2002 to help preserve the natural qualities of lands adjacent to the Appalachian Trail in Maine. It will focus future conservation efforts on the western mountains and the 100-Mile Wilderness area, two regions where much of the land is still unprotected from development.

Source: Northern Sky News (Elly Pepper)

Pondicherry Wildlife Refuge. This spectacular refuge northwest of the Presidential Range has grown again with the addition of a 309-acre tract last January and a 499-acre parcel last June, bringing the refuge total area to 5,304 acres, including 120 acres protected by conservation easement. The most recently acquired acreage is near the Mount Washington Regional Airport in Whitefield and includes Hazen Pond, several beaver ponds and other wetlands, and sections of the Johns River. It also protects part of the access trail into the refuge, which follows an old railbed. Both tracts were added with the assistance of the Nature Conservancy, and much of the funding came from

the purchase of migratory waterfowl permits, also known as "duck stamps."
Source: The Courier, Littleton, New Hampshire

Hardwood Ridge Tract Added to WMNF. Through the efforts of the Trust for Public Land (TPL), a 1,735-acre tract known as Hardwood Ridge, located in the town of Jefferson, has been added to the White Mountain National Forest (WMNF). The parcel borders the Israel River, and, according to Forest Supervisor Tom Wagner, public ownership will protect the water quality of tributary streams that flow into the Israel, helping meet the WMNF goal of watershed protection.

The acquisition also preserves recreational opportunities for hiking, fishing, hunting, trapping, and snowmobiling. Two major snowmobile corridor trails traverse the property, an east–west route linking Littleton and Gorham, and a north–south route that connects Lincoln and Twin Mountain with Berlin.

The area also features wetlands and riparian zones, providing habitat for Carex species, amphibians, waterfowl, and bats. It is also the site of important deer wintering habitat.
Source: TPL/WMNF Press Release

Forest Legacy Projects in Northern New Hampshire. Grants from the federally-funded Forest Legacy program have been used to help protect several important parcels in northern New Hampshire. A $2 million appropriation will allow the Town of Errol, north of the White Mountains, to purchase and manage more than 5,000 acres as a town forest. The town matched the grant with a $2.2 million bond. The acquired area, known as 13-Mile Woods, borders the Androscoggin River and is rich in wildlife habitat. Also appropriated were $1.5 million for land acquisition at Lake Umbagog National Wildlife Refuge; $1.5 million for land at Mirror Lake in Thornton, adjacent to the important ecological research center at Hubbard Brook Experimental Forest; and $1.2 million for the acquisition of 2,660 acres around Trout Pond in Freedom, in the eastern Lakes Region. The tract in Freedom is adjacent to over 2,000 acres of existing conservation land.
Source: Forest Notes (Society for the Protection of New Hampshire Forests)

—Steven D. Smith
"News and Notes" Editor

Books of Note

Savage Summit
The True Stories of the First Five Women Who Climbed K2.
By Jennifer Jordan.
New York, William Morrow, 2005.
Illustrated. 303 pp. ISBN: 006-058-7156. Price: $24.95 (hardcover).

IN A RECENT INTERVIEW in *The New York Times* (June 18, 2005, p. D5), Ed Viesturs, the first American to summit all fourteen of the world's peaks over 26,000 feet high, described the challenge of the "death zone" as follows: "It's one of the few places in the world where no one can come and get you. You're so dependent on your own decisions. Every decision has a consequence. It's not that I like to tempt fate, but I like to see what I can do and can't do." I believe that this quotation provides a framework for understanding the challenge and risk that each of the five women profiled in Jennifer Jordan's thrilling account set for herself as she climbed K2.

Jordan, herself a climber, writer, producer, and radio commentator, opens Savage Summit by explaining her own journey to this story and the questions she posed and strove to answer: Why did each woman choose to flirt with death by entering the death zone? Why did she "revel" in the experience? Why did one mountain claim three of their lives on the descent (the other two died on subsequent climbs)? How did they make the decision to leave husbands, lovers, and children behind? Did their gender play a role in their deaths? Jordan spent six years researching; reading the women's journals; and interviewing family members, friends, and previous biographers.

In 1986, Polish climber Wanda Rutkiewicz (1943–92) was the first woman to summit K2, followed later that year by French climber Liliane Barrard (1948–86) and British alpinist Julie Tullis (1939–86), both of whom died on their descent. In 1992 French climber Chantal Mauduit (1964–98) summited K2, and finally in 1995 British climber Alison Hargreaves (1962–95) reached the summit but died early in her descent. While each woman's story is somewhat different, there are basic similarities: each woman was drawn, even addicted, to climbing at a very young age and became passionate about her pursuit; each worked extraordinarily hard mastering her skills; each faced the criticism and sometimes outright discrimination of male climbers who doubted their abilities and/or who needed to help them physically achieve their goals; and each was ultimately a loner and a narcissist, a woman who put ambition before family, friends, and self-preservation. For these women, there was no choice; as the author writes about Chantal Mauduit, "At fifteen, she realized what many people never do: everyone is going to die, so she might as well live a passionate life while she was here." From Jordan's extensive research, I believe it is accurate to say that each woman lived as she needed to live and died as she would have chosen to die.

While Jordan isn't really able to answer all the research questions she poses in her introduction, she has written a fascinating and disturbing book about five courageous women, a book that may leave the reader with more questions than answers. Perhaps we must be content to conclude with Viesturs that devoting a lifetime to the challenge of conquering a place so immense that it takes all of one's physical, mental, emotional, and spiritual capabilities just to survive, let alone surmount, is worth the ultimate risk.

—*Pamela Miller Ness*

Rogue River Journal

A Winter Alone.
By John Daniel.
Washington, D.C., Shoemaker & Hoard, 2005.
352 pp. ISBN: 159-376-0515. Price: $26.00 (hardcover).

CERTAIN MALES TEST THEMSELVES WITH SOLITUDE. They take the questioning—and perhaps questionable—"I" off to some remote area and set to figuring him out. The writerly members of this tribe often approach such sojourns with a packful of journals and dispatches from predecessors. From their solitary outposts, they observe the world they have joined and reflect on the one they have left. Paradoxically, from this singularity they often discover the relationships that define them. Alone, they become more deeply connected to the people and places of their lives.

So it is with John Daniel in his vivid new book, *Rogue River Journal*, a memoir set in Daniel's fifty-second year and in the winter-closed, isolate valley of that Oregon river. For four and a half months, Daniel lives alone at a camp maintained as a writer's retreat. He takes along a mountain of food and his ranging memory. Packed away in his haul of accompaniment are boxes of family correspondence and a hefty portion of Henry Thoreau's writings. He also carries compromise, in the form of a radio phone with which he phones in a weekly "I'm-okay-here's-the-news" to his wife, Marilyn, who by arrangement is not home to answer his call.

The book that emerges from Daniel's 127-day sojourn is rich in understanding of a man's primary wilderness—himself. Because Daniel, who is also a poet, knows the weight and shape of words, this is a book to be savored. There is enough meditation on Daniel's days alone and the Rogue River canyon to offer readers a sense of that immediate experience, but the book's real exploration happens in deep family thickets. In particular, Daniel bushwhacks into the dense backcountry of his relationship with his father, the charismatic labor organizer, Franz Daniel, and then necessarily into the company of surrogate fathers he finds along the way of his growing up. "If a boy is lucky," Daniel points out, "he has several fathers, and some of them have to be very unlike himself." A little later, he writes, "A boy wants to become a man, and needs to become a man, even as he fights it as hard as he can every step."

Daniel, like many of his generation, waged a long fight against growing into manhood; some of the battles were fought directly with his father, most were fought solo against manifestations of the world's paternity. A Presidential Scholar in high school, Daniel dropped out of college, refused the military at the height of the Vietnam draft, sought the alternative space of a drugged counter-culture, found initial work in the woods and then discovered rock climbing. Through it all, he gradually fashioned a self at a writer's table. Finally, with help and through words, he becomes his own father.

But before that happens fully, Daniel must acknowledge, understand, and then leave his other fathers, at least symbolically. In one of the most beautiful passages in this book, he imagines his father and mother where they were happiest, out for the evening along New Orleans' streets, an evening from which they emerge with a talismanic checked tablecloth that Daniel will see throughout his childhood. "And so," he writes, "I say good-bye to them. I have followed them closely for several years now, each of them alone and the two together. I have looked after their lives, eager for all scraps I could find, and now I am ready to let them go. As their figures recede in the warm New Orleans' twilight, mixing with the other walkers, I imagine that my father with his arm around my mother looks once behind him. I see him but he does not see me, and as his face turns forward again it's as though a great fish, having been fought into the shallows of a river, suddenly feels its freedom and turns away into the dim green depths."

On one level, the great fish is Daniel's father. But clearly, the freed fish also is John Daniel.

— Sandy Stott

Snowstruck

In the Grip of Avalanches.
By Jill Fredston.
New York, Harcourt, 2005.
352 pp. ISBN: 015-101-2490. Price: $24.00 (hardcover).

SNOWSTRUCK'S CHAPTER THREE OPENS with a photo of a long chain of people ascending Alaska's wintry Chilkoot Pass. Soon the reader learns that everyone in the photo is doing "the Chilkoot Lockstep," an uphill shuffle to the top of the pass and a chance at joining the 1898 gold rush into Alaska's Klondike. But a reader who knows snow might be pardoned for wondering what all those people were doing tramping together across a slope that looks distinctly like avalanche terrain. Seeking fortune, would be the ready answer, but of course those who seek gold often find hard lessons rather than wealth, and most of these Klondike stampeders found hardship in abundance. Later in the chapter, woe visits in the form of one of history's deadliest avalanches, wiping out tens of stampeders.

The story of these Klondike aspirants is uncovered by one of *Snowstruck's* central characters, snow and avalanche guru Doug Fesler, who also happens to be the author's husband (their romance is a subplot of this larger love affair with snow). Fesler is digging back through old newspapers to learn more of avalanche history in Alaska, the couple's home state. It is a measure of his and the book's focus on avalanches that he will closet himself in small, dark rooms to read microfilms about snow sliding a hundred years ago. Fesler's rediscovery of the intimate knowledge about the natural world that Alaska's aboriginal people once enjoyed makes him a valuable anachronism, albeit one who use modern analytic tools. Fesler and Fredston remind us in lucid detail of what is lost when we march in lockstep pursuit of wealth and away from a right relationship with nature. We might as well be crossing a perilous slope poised to carry us all away.

— Sandy Stott

Alpine Climbing

Techniques to Take You Higher.
By Mark Houston and Kathy Cosley.
Seattle, The Mountaineers Books, 2004.
326 pp. ISBN: 089-886-7495. Price: $24.95 (paperback).

THIS BOOK IS AN IMPORTANT CONTRIBUTION to the literature of American mountaineering and can be compared to such predecessors as Ken Henderson's *Handbook of American Mountaineering* (Houghton Mifflin Co., Boston, 1942), *Belaying the Leader*, by Leonard et al. (The Sierra Club, San Francisco, 1956), and *The Mountaineers' Mountaineering: Freedom of the Hills*, First Edition (Seattle, 1961).

Alpine Climbing is a text aimed at intermediate climbers who have already learned many of the basic climbing skills but now want to go higher. Though it is about alpine style climbing, it is not intended to prepare the reader for expedition climbing of the highest mountains—those more than about 6,000 meters.

Throughout their book, Houston and Cosley stress safety. I was pleased to see a Mountaineers' publication devote the initial chapter to decision-making and risk. Even the latest edition of *Mountaineering: Freedom of the Hills* (7th Edition, 2003) has only a page or two devoted to the issue of decision-making, and a short chapter on leadership that is concerned mostly with leadership style and the mechanics of leadership. John Graham's *Outdoor Leadership: Technique, Common Sense, & Self-Confidence* (The Mountaineers Books, 1997), does contain a chapter on decision-making, but it is not a book on climbing.

Devoting their text primarily to the French and Swiss Alps, the authors have little to say about climbing in the northeastern United States. They suggest that insulated leather boots should be adequate for ice and mixed climbs in this area. (They may not have climbed in the White Mountains at minus 20 degrees) They do not discuss wind slab and its dangers, and they dismiss compass declination, saying that it is zero in the Swiss Alps. There is an emphasis on traveling fast to assure safety and accomplishing speed by leaving bivouac gear behind. There is no mention of emergency shelters, such as snow caves. On the other hand, they do extol the virtues of their 8-ounce double bivouac sack.

As a radio amateur operator, I was surprised to find that the authors suggest acquiring amateur licenses and the use of two-meter handheld transceivers, because of their light weight and the many mountaintop repeaters. What they don't explain is that most of those repeaters (at least in the Northeast) operate in duplex mode (different receiving and transmitting frequencies) and require a specific sound beep to access. Programming a transceiver needs to be done in advance of a climb.

In comparison with the recent edition of MFOTH, *Alpine Climbing* is 250 pages shorter and many topics do not receive as much coverage, but it is aimed at those who have learned the basics. *Alpine Climbing* has pictures of climbing techniques, whereas MFOTH relies on line drawings. There are many sidebars about real climbing situations. The authors do state their preferences, while MFOTH was written with editorial objectivity.

In spite of what I see as certain drawbacks, I do recommend this book, and I urge the authors in their second edition to address issues such as compass declination, wind slabs, the potential severity of climbing in the Northeast, and the programming of two-meter transceivers.

— *Dan H. Allen*

Walking the Big Wild

From Yellowstone to the Yukon on the Grizzly Bear's Trail.
By Karsten Heuer.
Seattle, The Mountaineers Books, 2005.
258 pp. ISBN: 0-89866-983-8. Price: $16.95 (paperback).

WHEN INTERSTATE 78 WAS BUILT in Eastern New Jersey, several strange overpasses appeared, wider than most and paved with plants, not concrete. These were "wildlife corridors," intended to provide continuous passage for animal life otherwise isolated by the interstate barrier. But a meters-wide passageway, perhaps adequate for rabbits, squirrels, and suburbanized deer, will hardly do for the larger omnivores, like bears, or for the much rarer carnivores at the top of the food chain. These animals' larger ranges require contiguous areas no longer available in the East and becoming scarce in the West. Karsten Heuer's journey is a quest to follow one of the remaining such corridors and to promote its value.

Alternately following established trails and animal tracks and bushwacking, Heuer makes his way with his various companions (the most steady of whom is his trusty dog, Webster), along the spine of the northern Rockies. His wildlife encounters are many, including bear, moose, caribou, and the elusive wolverine, whose tracks prove the most reliable indicator of the easiest path through trailless territory. Heuer is a skilled and experienced backcountry traveler, and his trek is fun to follow.

Between stretches of hiking, Heuer has arranged meetings in towns to promote the concept of Y2Y, the Yellowstone to Yukon Conservation Initiative. Designed to link existing preserves with wildlife corridors, the proposal arouses the opposition of some interests, notably the logging industry and its labor force, which already feel threatened by conservationists. Yet Heuer is convinced that if he is allowed to present his program, which includes sustainable uses of natural resources, the reception will ultimately be positive. His quest is to halt the sprawl that threatens to choke off the corridor, isolating animal populations.

Walking the Big Wild is two books in one. For those who enjoy a good armchair adventure in the wilderness and those who find the prospect of preservation on this ambitious a scale uplifting, it is a recommended read.

—*Paul M. Ness*

A Peak Ahead

In 1987. when i was 28, I resigned from my job as a harried editor to hike the Appalachian Trail with my husband and two friends. I left a life in which people you met always asked, "What do you do?" For four and a half months, all we did was hike, and the mountains didn't care if we succeeded or not. I cried every day on the trail. But I had changed, and forever.

It wasn't just that I had lived without an address. And I certainly did not emerge as an all-knowing woodlands goddess. I remain a slightly fearful person who learned to make an arduous journey and to live outdoors. Because I lived for so long outdoors that year, the woods became the normal setting, where I'd always prefer to be.

I don't mean that I now want to live in a cave, but that I appreciate how to move forward in life. The trail also made me understand Earth's abundance. The weather is not a backdrop for recreation. It provides water and food so that we survive. If I'm outside, in touch with the weather, I feel at home. If I'm stuck in a building for too long, I feel cut off.

The readers of *Appalachia* share a respect for nature and the simple truths it delivers. In the mountains, we learn how to press on. We learn survival, caring, humility, fortutude, and patience.

Becoming the editor of this journal, a dream of mine, has joined the journalist in me to the hiker in me for the first time in two decades.

My first issue of *Appalachia*, the 222nd, will come out in June. Writers will consider what hikers gain when we pull ourselves out of regular life to hike in the mountains, however briefly, and how those forays change us.

A former Zealand Falls hutmaster will describe the hut guests he met who yearned for the outdoors; he will consider why people don't connect as much with nature back home. An engineer will describe a whirlwind trek he crammed into his business trip to India—the peak was not what he expected. Veteran *Appalachia* writer Gene Daniell will write about the return to regular life of Ed Viesturs, the first American to climb all fourteen of the 8,000-meter peaks.

In the mountains, we confront our human weaknesses and learn when to step back from danger. Come join us next June, when we ask how to continue those journeys along the asphalt and floor-tile paths of cities and towns.

— Christine Woodside, Editor, cwoodside@snet.net

Submission Guidelines

Appalachia is a mountaineering and conservation journal published twice a year (June and December) by the Appalachian Mountain Club, 5 Joy Street, Boston, MA 02108. Nonprofit. Format: 6 x 9 inches. Founded 1876. Circulation: approximately 14,000.

Editor-in-Chief: Christine Woodside. Poetry Editor: Parkman Howe.

Appalachia welcomes nonfiction submissions and queries on the following topics: hiking; trekking; rock climbing; canoeing and kayaking; nature; mountain history and lore; and conservation. We recommend reading a sample issue before submitting. Samples are available at the above address for $10 per copy (postage included). Please enclose a SASE with all submissions.

Poetry: Original poems about the above topics are also welcome. Shorter poems are preferred. Only eight poems are published per issue, which makes this the most competitive section of the journal; on average, one in fifty submissions is accepted.

Artwork: Photographs or drawings accompany most of our articles and are usually provided by the authors. We also publish a limited number of stand-alone photos that evoke the mountains and welcome high-quality freelance submissions.

Deadlines: Writers should submit unsolicited material no later than January 15 for the Summer/Fall issue, and no later than July 15 for the Winter/Spring issue. Because we publish only twice per year, writers should understand that accepted pieces might appear anywhere from six to eighteen months after acceptance.

Format: Articles generally run between 500 and 3,000 words and must be typed and double-spaced. Electronic submissions are welcome and may be sent to the editor-in-chief at: cwoodside@snet.net.

Editing: All work is subject to editing. We make every effort to review editing decisions with authors in the early stages of production, but deadlines make last-minute communication with authors impossible.

Payment: As a nonprofit journal, we cannot pay for unsolicited material. Authors receive two contributor copies.

Web publication: Excerpts from each issue are routinely published on AMC's website, www.outdoors.org, after the issue has been mailed.